Cambridge El

G000081118

Elements in Metaphysics
edited by
Tuomas E. Tahko
University of Bristol

TIME

Heather Dyke
University of Otago

CAMBRIDGE
UNIVERSITY PRESS

CAMBRIDGE
UNIVERSITY PRESS

University Printing House, Cambridge CB2 8BS, United Kingdom

One Liberty Plaza, 20th Floor, New York, NY 10006, USA

477 Williamstown Road, Port Melbourne, VIC 3207, Australia

314–321, 3rd Floor, Plot 3, Splendor Forum, Jasola District Centre,
New Delhi – 110025, India

103 Penang Road, #05–06/07, Visioncrest Commercial, Singapore 238467

Cambridge University Press is part of the University of Cambridge.

It furthers the University's mission by disseminating knowledge in the pursuit of
education, learning, and research at the highest international levels of excellence.

www.cambridge.org
Information on this title: www.cambridge.org/9781108940726
DOI: 10.1017/9781108935517

First published 2021

A catalogue record for this publication is available from the British Library.

ISBN 978-1-108-94072-6 Paperback
ISSN 2633-9862 (online)
ISSN 2633-9854 (print)

Time

Elements in Metaphysics

DOI: 10.1017/9781108935517
First published online: December 2021

Heather Dyke
University of Otago

Author for correspondence: Heather Dyke, heather.dyke@otago.ac.nz

Abstract: Philosophical thinking about time is characterised by tensions among competing conceptions. Different sources of evidence yield different conclusions about it. Common sense suggests there is an objective present and that time is dynamic. Science recognises neither feature. This Element examines McTaggart's argument for the unreality of time, which epitomises this tension, showing how it gave rise to the A-theory/B-theory debate. Each theory is in tension with either ordinary or scientific thinking so must accommodate the competing conception. Reconciling the A-theory with science does not look promising. Prospects look better for the B-theory's attempt to accommodate ordinary thinking about time.

Keywords: time, tense, McTaggart, A-theory, B-theory

ISBNs: 9781108940726 (PB), 9781108935517 (OC)
ISSNs: 2633-9862 (online), 2633-9854 (print)

Contents

1 What Is Puzzling about Time? 1

2 Methodology in the Philosophy of Time 4

3 McTaggart and His Legacy 12

4 The A-Theory 26

5 The B-Theory 38

6 Explaining Temporal Experience 51

7 Concluding Remarks 67

References 68

1 What Is Puzzling about Time?

Philosophers have perennially expressed puzzlement when thinking about time. Perhaps most famously, St Augustine wondered, 'What, then, is time? If no one asks me, I know; but, if I want to explain it to a questioner, I do not know' (Augustine, 1953: 343). Other examples abound. But what exactly is so puzzling about time? The quote from St Augustine suggests that time is at once familiar and banal, and yet also mysterious and elusive. Most of us will, I think, recognise the conflict alluded to here. But how can time be both familiar and banal, yet also mysterious and elusive?

Time seems to pervade our entire existence, and our experience of it has a particular quality. Every experience we have, our innermost thoughts, our mundane activities, our achievement of lifetime goals, all are located within time. All stand in some temporal relation to every other event in our lives and, indeed, to every other event in the history of the universe. As well as being located within time, our experiences come with a distinctive felt presentness. I am not just experiencing typing at my computer; I am experiencing typing at my computer *now* – so too for all my other experiences, whenever they occur. In short, all of our experiences have a uniquely temporal character. But on the other hand, time does not appear to be an object of experience. I do not perceive or observe time. The closest I come to experiencing time is through experiencing change. I perceive the second hand moving around a clock face; I hear the notes of a melody; I see a yellow banana in the fruit bowl, remembering that it was once green. These are experiences of ordinary change. Time seems to be a necessary condition for ordinary change to occur, but it is not, prima facie, the same thing as ordinary change. So time seems to be all-pervasive and yet curiously elusive. In response to this source of puzzlement, some philosophers have sought to identify the elusive time with something more directly observable, such as change.

Another source of puzzlement about time arises out of a tension between two ways in which we think of events as situated in time. Events are laid out in a temporal order, all related to each other by the temporal relations, *earlier than*, *later than* and *simultaneous with*. Which of those events are happening now depends on where in that temporal manifold we ourselves are located. But we also think of events as coming to be and passing away. My present typing will soon be past, and my future coffee break will instead be present. But how, if events are laid out in a temporal manifold, can they also come to be and pass away?

Philosophical reactions to this source of puzzlement have been many and varied. Some have taken it to demonstrate that the notion of time is genuinely paradoxical, so time must be unreal. Others have attempted to resolve what they see as the mere appearance of paradox, arguing that time is real and not paradoxical. Within this class there are many different views on the precise nature of real, non-paradoxical time. We can see here a tendency towards both idealism and realism about time, while those who seek to identify time with change adopt a kind of reductionism about it.

In the face of this second source of puzzlement, which I will call the tension between being and becoming, realist philosophers who affirm the existence of time generally accept that the tension is real and that in order to resolve it they must choose whether time is better characterised in terms of being or becoming. Some choose being, arguing that becoming is best explained as some kind of illusion, projection or aspect of mere appearance. Others choose becoming, arguing that everything is in flux, and that it is a mistake to think of time in terms of a fixed manifold of events.

A dispute of this kind was first articulated by the ancient Greeks. The Eleatic school, whose proponents included Parmenides and Zeno, noted a distinction between appearances and reality; how things appear can deceive us into a false apprehension of how things really are. They argued that change is one element of misleading appearances and is therefore unreal. Since time is necessary for change, it too is unreal. The Eleatics thus took the idealist path in response to the tension between being and becoming. Opposed to the Eleatics was Heraclitus and his followers, who argued that everything is radically in flux. Change and becoming are not paradoxical. Instead, the attempt to grasp becoming in language is what gives rise to paradox. Language, which requires permanence in meaning, will inevitably misrepresent a world in which there is no permanence. The Heracliteans thus opted for one version of realism, prioritising becoming and rejecting the charge that time itself is paradoxical.[1]

A more recent articulation of this tension appears in the work of British idealist J. M. E. McTaggart (1908, 1927) and has given rise to much of the debate in the philosophy of time over the last century. According to McTaggart, the notion of events laid out in a temporal order is inadequate to capture the true nature of time. For that we must appeal to the notion of events coming to be and passing away. And yet, for McTaggart, there is a paradox lurking within this notion of temporal becoming. Temporal becoming is therefore both essential to time and inherently paradoxical, so time itself does not exist.

In this Element I propose to diagnose this puzzlement as stemming from a deeper tension: a tension between two philosophical tendencies that pull us in different directions in our quest to understand the world. These are, first,

---

[1] For more on the dispute between the Eleatics and the Heracliteans, see Bardon (2013).

to understand the world as it is in itself, independently of us – a third-person conception of the world. This tendency characterises philosophical investigations into such topics as the nature of matter and substance, space and causation. It also characterises much scientific investigation, such as physics and astronomy. I call this the tendency to subject-neutral understanding. Second, we have a tendency to want to understand the world as it appears to us, from our distinctively human perspective – a first-person conception of the world. This tendency characterises philosophical investigations into such topics as the nature of free will, agency and knowledge. But it too characterises much scientific investigation, such as psychology, cognitive science and neuroscience. I call this the tendency to subject-relative understanding.

These two tendencies drive much philosophical investigation but can give rise to conflict. Sometimes, as the Eleatics observed, our understanding of the world as it appears to us conflicts with our understanding of the world as it is independently of us. This is particularly true, I argue, of time. Our aim should be to resolve this tension by achieving an understanding of time as it is independently of us, which also accommodates and explains our experience of, and perspective on, time.

Having alluded to the classification of idealist, realist and reductionist approaches to time, the majority of this Element will focus on two particular versions of realism that emerged in the twentieth century. One version, the A-theory,[2] prioritises becoming over being. Time, on this view, divides objectively into past, present and future and is dynamic. Events change from being future, to present, to past. The A-theory attempts to do justice to our ordinary experience of, and beliefs about, time and so prioritises the tendency to subject-relative understanding.

The other version, the B-theory, prioritises being over becoming. Time, on this view, is characterised by the temporal relations, *earlier than*, *later than* and *simultaneous with*, that obtain between moments and events. There is no objective distinction between past, present and future, and time is not dynamic, on this view. The fact that we draw this distinction says more about us than it does about time. Instead, events and times stand in fixed, unchanging temporal relations to each other. There is no temporal becoming, only temporal being. The B-theory attempts to do justice to time as it is in itself, without reference to our first-person experience of it, prioritising the tendency to subject-neutral understanding.

---

[2] The terms 'A-theory' and 'B-theory' derive from the work of McTaggart. I explain McTaggart's argument, and this terminology, in Section 3.

Here is the roadmap for the rest of this Element. In Section 2 I consider the methodological issue of how best to go about investigating the nature of time. I argue that the best approach, which will accommodate both philosophical tendencies, is a multidisciplinary one involving the findings of science and philosophy. In Section 3 I expound McTaggart's seminal work in the philosophy of time and show how the debate between the A-theory and the B-theory emerged out if it. Sections 4 and 5 examine arguments for and against the A-theory and the B-theory, respectively. The result of this examination is that the most promising theory of the metaphysical nature of time is the B-theory, so the remainder of the Element focuses on exploring ways in which the B-theory can respond to the chief criticism it faces. That is, the B-theory owes us an explanation of why, if there is no objective present and no temporal becoming, we seem to experience it as if there are. Section 6 examines B-theoretic attempts to provide this explanation. Section 7 concludes.

2 Methodology in the Philosophy of Time

How should we go about investigating the fundamental, metaphysical nature of time? First, we should consider what the ultimate goal is of such an enquiry. Plausibly, it is to arrive at an account of the nature of time that is objectively true – that tells us the truth about time from a universal standpoint, not merely from a local, perspectival or human-centred point of view. How might we arrive at such an account? One source of knowledge about the nature of reality that philosophers, particularly those of an empiricist leaning, have traditionally appealed to is our experience of that reality. Another is scientific investigation. So what can these two sources of knowledge tell us about the nature of time?

2.1 A Folk Theory of Time

As we saw in Section 1, human experience is shot through with temporality. But we can identify within that experience a number of distinctive characteristics that we pre-theoretically ascribe to time. Call this our 'folk theory' of time.[3] First, our experiences take place in the present. One moment is uniquely marked out from all others as present, and it seems to be a shared present moment such

---

[3] I am not claiming that all humans necessarily possess such a theory or would necessarily assent to the claims I am about to introduce. Rather, I am suggesting a broad-brush picture of time that has proved remarkably persistent in both philosophical and non-philosophical thinking about time over the centuries. Whether, and to what extent, individuals in the general population would assent to these claims is an interesting empirical question. Some work towards answering it and related questions has been initiated by Latham et al. (2020a, 2020b and 2021) and Shardlow et al. (2021). As we will see in Section 6, some philosophers argue that elements of the folk theory introduced here misdescribe the nature of our temporal experience.

that it appears to be universal or somehow privileged. By contrast, each of us occupies a different spatial location, which can be referred to as 'here'. Where *here* is, is not a universal feature of space but is relative to one's spatial perspective. But when *now* or *the present* is does not seem to be relative to one's temporal perspective in the same way. I will call this first feature that we ascribe to time on the basis of experience 'the privileged present'.

As soon as we articulate the privileged present, a further feature of time suggests itself. Simply describing a privileged present fails to completely capture our temporal experience. If we stopped there we would have described a fixed, static designation of one moment as the present. We would have failed to acknowledge that which moment that is, and which events it contains, keeps changing. Time is not constituted by a fixed and static distribution of events and moments into past, present and future. Instead, that distribution is continually changing. This feature of time is intended to be captured by such metaphorical expressions as 'the relentless march of time' and 'the flow of time'. As Donald Williams remarks,

> [t]ime flows or flies or marches, years roll, hours pass. More explicitly we may speak as if the perceiving mind were stationary while time flows by like a river, with the flotsam of events upon it; or as if presentness were a fixed pointer under which the tape of happenings slides; or as if the time sequence were a moving-picture film, unwinding from the dark reel of the future, projected briefly on the screen of the present, and rewound into the dark can of the past. (Williams, 1951: 461)

I will call this feature that we ascribe to time on the basis of experience 'temporal passage'.

These two components of our folk theory of time are intended to be characterisations of how things seem to us, temporally, that are neutral among competing theoretical views about the nature of time. They are elements of our folk theory that stand in need of explanation by any metaphysical theory of the nature of time. I take these two features to be the central components of our folk theory of time, while acknowledging that there are others. For example, we also ordinarily think that time has a direction and that there is a fundamental asymmetry between the past and the future.

2.2 Scientific Thinking about Time

Our temporal experience, together with a little reflection on it, thus furnishes us with a folk theory of time. What of the alternative source of knowledge about time? What does science tell us time is like? The scientific discipline most suited to providing a theory of the nature of time is physics, but physics does not constitute a fixed body of knowledge. Consequently, what physics tells us about time has undergone change over time. Even now, we lack a unified picture of physical time. Nevertheless, there has always been a prima facie tension between physical time and our folk theory of time (Callender, 2017: 19). Crucially, the features of time according to our folk theory, or what Callender (2017) calls 'manifest time', have never figured in any physical theory about the nature of time.

> Aristotelian physics, Newtonian physics, Einsteinian physics, and quantum mechanics all manage without positing a special now. Lacking a now, they don't posit a temporal flow or a past/future asymmetry either, as both are dependent on a now. (Callender, 2017: 21)

To illustrate, let's look briefly at how one of our best confirmed current scientific theories of time, the special theory of relativity (STR), manages without positing a special now.[4] According to STR, whether or not two events are simultaneous depends on the perspective, or frame of reference, of an observer. From one perspective, two space-like separated events, e_1 and e_2, may be simultaneous, but from another e_1 is earlier than e_2, and from another, e_1 is later than e_2. Furthermore, according to STR, there is no way of picking out one of these perspectives as more privileged, absolute or 'correct' than any of the others. Thus, there is no objective fact about whether e_1 is simultaneous with e_2. There are only frame-relative facts about simultaneity. But if there are only relative facts about simultaneity, it follows that there are only relative facts about which events are present and hence also about which events are past and future. According to STR then, there can be no objective (frame-independent) division of events into past, present and future. But that is precisely what is required for there to be an objective present moment. And to the extent that it is dependent on there being an objective present moment, temporal passage is also inconsistent with STR.

Thus, we have an apparent clash between what we think is true of the world based on our tendency to subject-neutral understanding and what we think is true of it based on our tendency to subject-relative understanding. Taken at face value, these two pictures of reality conflict: is there a special now or not? Does time flow or not?

What should we do in the face of this apparent conflict? The options seem to be the following: (1) Argue that physics is wrong to exclude features of time as we experience it. This does not seem a particularly promising route. As Conee

---

[4] We might go further, as many have (Rietdijk 1966; Putnam 1967; Penrose 1989; Sider 2001; Saunders 2002; Gibson and Pooley 2008; Leininger 2021), and argue that STR is *inconsistent* with positing a special now.

and Sider (2014: 124) remark, '[o]ne's philosophy should avoid colliding with or limiting science'. (2) Argue that the features of time as we experience it can be explained away as some kind of illusion or mere appearance. I examine some attempts to run this line in Section 6. But it is worth stating at the outset that this approach too seems problematic. That we are subject to such a widespread and all-encompassing illusion itself cries out for explanation. (3) Find some way of preserving and integrating both views. The view that I will be recommending attempts to take this third route.

2.3 The Linguistic Approach to the Philosophy of Time

Before outlining my preferred methodology in the attempt to resolve this conflict, it's worth reflecting on the methodology that was employed in the metaphysics of time for much of the second half of the twentieth century. That approach placed considerable emphasis on temporal features of natural language. Those who took time to be more or less accurately described by our folk theory of time pointed to the fact that the language we use to talk about the world presupposes those features (Prior, 1967; Gale, 1968; Smith, 1993; Ludlow, 1999; Craig, 2000). Language recognises a distinction between past, present and future, and this 'tensedness' is built into its very structure. In English, and many other natural languages, it is built into the grammatical structure. Other languages have different syntactic and semantic means of locating events within this tensed manifold, but it is generally accepted that all languages have some means of doing this, and to that extent, all languages are tensed (Sinha & Gärdenfors, 2014: 4). Proponents of this view then argued that tensed language captures and expresses the true, tensed nature of reality and does so irreducibly. Any attempt to describe reality without using tensed language would result in an impoverished, false description that omits an essential feature of reality: the fact that it is tensed.

Opponents of this view rejected the claim that language is irreducibly tensed. They argued that tensed sentences can be reduced to, or translated by, tenseless sentences that posit temporal relations between events and moments of speech (Russell, 1915; Goodman, 1951; Quine, 1960; Smart, 1963). For example, the tensed sentence 'The inauguration of Joe Biden is past,' uttered in February 2021, can be reduced to, or translated by, some tenseless sentence such as 'The inauguration of Joe Biden occurs (tenselessly) earlier than February 2021.' These attempts at reduction or translation acknowledge that tensed sentences are perspectival – they are only true at certain times – but offer a tenseless sentence that attempts to capture, and make explicit, that perspectival information. The result is a sentence that can be truly uttered at any time and so is not, itself, perspectival. The motivation for this approach was to show that, while language is tensed, it is not essentially so, and therefore, it does not follow that there is some feature of reality that it uniquely refers to.

Debate in the philosophy of time proceeded to focus on whether tensed language could be, or could not be, eliminated or reduced to tenseless language. Developments in the philosophy of language, however, established that tense, like other forms of indexicality, is in fact irreducible in the sense at issue in this debate (Castañeda, 1967; Perry, 1979; Kaplan, 1989). Tense cannot be eliminated from language without losing the ability to convey certain information. But this did not settle the debate in favour of those who believe reality is tensed. Their opponents changed tack and argued that, while tense in language may be irreducible, it doesn't follow that reality too is tensed. Instead, true and irreducibly tensed sentences have tenseless truth conditions or truthmakers (Smart, 1980; Mellor, 1981, 1998; Oaklander, 1984; Le Poidevin, 1991).

The shift in focus from eliminating tense in language to arguing that temporal reality need not be tensed to account for it constituted a move from linguistic to metaphysical concerns. Nevertheless, the debate still placed a surprising emphasis on the nature of language, given that the goal of the enquiry is to investigate the fundamental, metaphysical nature of time (Heil, 2005; Dyke, 2008; Taylor, 2019). Linguistics is inherently neutral with respect to the metaphysical nature of reality (Taylor, 2019: 33–34). This neutrality is rooted in the fact that semantics is an enquiry into the mind and its representational powers, not into the nature of the external world or the relation between mind and world. And this is just as we should expect. One function of language is to represent the world, so investigating language can at most reveal facts about our representational faculties – how we think about the world.

Taylor (2019) identifies two approaches to metaphysical enquiry: the way of ideas and the way of reference. The way of ideas begins by interrogating and sharpening the ideational contents of our concepts. Once we have sharpened our concepts of, for example, virtue, number, time, freedom or water, we are in a position to say what something must be like to be an instance of virtue, number, time, freedom or water. The linguistic approach to the philosophy of time is clearly an instance of the way of ideas (Dyke, 2021b). It recommends analysing the language we use to represent temporal reality and drawing metaphysical conclusions about temporal reality from that analysis.

Taylor has a number of arguments against the way of ideas. He notes that even its most committed adherents must accept that it is possible that there is nothing in the world that answers to some concept. At some point, a priori interrogation of our concepts must 'give way to a degree of a posteriori empirical inquiry into what there really is' (Taylor, 2019: 51). Merely attending to our concepts and representations of reality 'in which we meet with nothing extra-representational [could not] possibly suffice to give us access to a realm of free-standing objects' (Taylor, 2019: 86). The way of ideas fails to forge a link between our representations and the reality they represent so leaves us trapped within the realm of representations.

A second argument appeals to what Taylor calls 'problematically related domains of entities' (Taylor, 2019: 64). He cites examples: 'the normative and the natural; qualitative states of consciousness and neurophysiological states of the brain' (Taylor, 2019: 64), but think also of the tensed and the tenseless. These pairs of domains are problematic in that it is not obvious how the concepts in one domain are related to the concepts in the other. If one approaches this issue deploying the way of ideas, one will ask whether, for example, tensed concepts are reducible to tenseless concepts. Accepting the reducibility of tensed concepts encourages the thought that only the concepts in the reductive base, tenseless concepts, have correlates in reality, so there are no tensed properties. Rejecting the reducibility of tensed concepts encourages the thought that there are properties out there in the world, namely, tensed properties, which are the correlates of tensed concepts. But this line of reasoning should be resisted. Arguments that lead to metaphysical conclusions about the constituents of reality on the basis of the distinctness or otherwise of conceptual domains are, at the very least, hasty. Our employment of tensed concepts may not be reducible to our employment of tenseless concepts, but it does not follow that the facts in the world answering to those concepts must be distinctively tensed. Conceptual differences between these problematically related domains do not necessarily carry over to the metaphysical realm.

2.4 A Collaborative Approach to Metaphysical Enquiry

If the way of ideas in metaphysical enquiry is misleading, how might we deploy the way of reference instead? Taylor thinks our approach should be naturalistic, broadly continuous with science (Taylor, 2019: 5 n. 4) and collaborative. The task of 'limning the true and ultimate structure of reality' (Quine, 1960: 202) should be seen as the joint work of all forms of enquiry, not the preserve of metaphysics, physics or any of the special sciences (Taylor, 2019: 106). Callender (2017) agrees. He argues that the problem of reconciling what science tells us about the nature of time (physical time), with how time appears to us in experience (manifest time), requires a collaborative effort from science, physics in particular, but also psychology, physiology, neuroscience and evolutionary biology. Linguistics, semantics and logical analysis have their role to play too. Philosophy brings particular strengths to this interdisciplinary project, not least the ability to see past disciplinary boundaries, and tie the threads of the project together.

Taylor diagnoses the urge towards the way of ideas as symptomatic of the fear that philosophy will have nothing to contribute to metaphysical enquiry if it cannot be done a priori (Taylor, 2019: 106). Callender takes a similar view. He suggests that the emphasis, first on temporal semantics and then on temporal ontology, in the philosophy of time, came about in part as a response to the discipline's feeling increasingly threatened by science (Callender, 2017: 295). But the fear that scientific developments in this area make philosophy irrelevant is unwarranted. Philosophy and science can and should communicate with, inform and enlighten each other. Rovelli (2018) argues that philosophy has always had, and continues to have, a significant influence on science, physics in particular. Laplane et al. (2019) argue that there are at least four ways in which philosophy contributes to the progress of science. These are 'the clarification of scientific concepts, the critical assessment of scientific assumptions or methods, the formulation of new concepts and theories, and the fostering of dialogue between different sciences, as well as between science and society' (Laplane et al., 2019: 3949). This is not to say that philosophy is confined to the role of handmaiden to science, where all the significant advances are made. But recall the goal of a metaphysical enquiry into time. It is to investigate the fundamental nature of time. That is also the goal of scientific investigation into the nature of time. If these enquiries are carried out in isolation from each other, we have to wonder if they are really investigating the same thing.

Each of the roles for philosophy identified by Laplane et al. has its place in enquiries into the nature of time, but as that project becomes more interdisciplinary, the fourth one becomes particularly pertinent. One crucial role for philosophy in investigating the metaphysics of time is to navigate the interdisciplinary waters, tying together the disparate elements of these different enquiries all seeking to understand the same thing.

In the philosophy of time we must acknowledge both philosophical tendencies: to understand time as it is independently of us and as it appears to us in experience. Physics can make significant progress with the first. But we should not forget that our temporal experience is itself part of how the world objectively is and so stands in need of explanation, which should constitute part of our overall explanation of the nature of time. On these grounds, Goldman (2015) argues for a significant role for cognitive science in the metaphysical toolkit. He notes, '[M]etaphysicians appeal extensively to intuition, experience, and commonsense belief to guide their path in metaphysical theorizing' (Goldman, 2015: 174). But according to cognitive scientists, intuitions, perceptual experience and the beliefs based on them are all 'massively influenced by our cognitive system ... They are the products of complex computational operations, or neural circuits, which have formed over eons of evolutionary time' (Goldman, 2015: 174). We would therefore be remiss in our metaphysical enquiry if we did not incorporate facts about our cognitive system and how it generates intuitions, experience and commonsense beliefs.

Goldman's point is that facts about our cognition shape and contribute to our experience, so we should not simply assume that experience reliably indicates features of the external world. Just as we should not read our metaphysics off our language, we should not read it off our experience either. The nature of our experience, as well as intuitions and commonsense beliefs based on it, is a function of the nature of reality itself, together with the cognitive and perceptual systems that we employ in our interactions with reality. We could add in here features of our culture, and of our language (Dyke, 2021a), which also contribute to shaping our experience and thought about the world. Not paying sufficient attention to the role of our cognitive and perceptual systems, as well as the influence of culture and language, could lead us to misattribute properties to reality that are in fact generated by those systems and the way they interact with reality.

In her discussion of essentialism about natural kinds – of the kind defended by Putnam (1975) and Kripke (1980) – Leslie (2013) remarks, 'There are many explanations of why we may be fundamentally disposed to see the world in a particular way, only one of which is that *metaphysically or scientifically speaking, the world actually is that way*' (Leslie, 2013: 108). Like Goldman, she exhorts us not to read our metaphysics off our experience as there are many competing explanations for why our experience has the qualities that it does. An essentialist about natural kinds could respond by arguing that the explanation in question – that we are disposed to see the world in a particular way because, metaphysically or scientifically speaking, the world actually is that way – is not simply one of many competing explanations but, rather, is the best of the available explanations. The world seems to us to be a certain way, and the *best* explanation of this is that the world actually is that way. Such a response would need to be supported by reasons why this explanation is superior to other competing explanations. With respect to essentialism, however, Leslie also mounts a considerable battery of independent arguments to the conclusion that physical science fails to support it, giving us independent reason to doubt that it is the best explanation.

Leslie's approach to the debate about essentialism suggests a promising, parallel methodological approach for our enquiry into the nature of time. We should consider the deliverances of physical science on the nature of time, and we should also consider the deliverances of our experience. However, we should be aware that there are many alternative explanations of the nature of our temporal experience, only one of which is that, metaphysically or scientifically speaking, time really has the properties attributed to it by our folk theory of time. There may be independent explanations of the nature of our temporal experience that draw on facts about our cognitive and perceptual systems, our evolutionary history and our cultures and languages. Philosophy, in its role as navigator of the interdisciplinary waters, can marshal theories and evidence from disparate disciplines into one overarching theory of the nature of time.

2.5 Conclusion

Recall the goal of a metaphysical enquiry into the nature of time. We want an account of the nature of time that is objective – that describes time as it is independently of us, from a universal standpoint, and not merely from a perspectival standpoint. Scientific investigation clearly has a role to play in this enquiry, but a complete metaphysical enquiry will not end with the pronouncements of physics. Our cognitive and perceptual systems, our cultures and languages, all are part of objective reality, and they contribute to our experience of time in different ways. A complete account of the nature of time needs to incorporate explanations of these elements, and how they interact with observer-independent temporal reality to generate our experience of time. If scientific theories about time appear to conflict with what our experience tells us about time, we ought to aim to reconcile this conflict. One potentially fruitful way of doing this is to investigate all the factors that contribute to generating our experience. This approach, I believe, represents our best chance of doing justice to both philosophical tendencies: to understand time as it is in itself, and to understand it as it appears to us from our distinctively human perspective.

3 McTaggart and His Legacy

In Section 2 I introduced our folk theory of time. This is a theory of what time is like based on our ordinary temporal experience together with a minimal amount of reflection on that experience. It is made up of two central claims: (1) there is a privileged present moment, which marks a distinction between past, present and future, and (2) time is dynamic, in that which moment is present continually changes.[5] I also suggested that there is a tension between this folk theory and what we learn about the nature of time from science. Scientific thinking about time generally rejects the notion that there is a privileged present, and so also

---

[5] I am not suggesting that these two claims exhaust our folk theory of time. It may also include beliefs about, say, past-future asymmetry, or the direction of time. But I do think these two claims are central and essential to it.

rejects the further notions that depend on it, that there is an objective, observer-independent distinction between past, present and future and that time is dynamic with respect to this distinction. In this section I introduce the work of British idealist, John McTaggart Ellis McTaggart (1908, 1927) and show how it led to the emergence in the twentieth century of the dominant metaphysical views about time: the A-theory and the B-theory. These theories will be examined in Sections 4 and 5.

3.1 McTaggart's Argument for the Unreality of Time

McTaggart's influential argument was an argument for the unreality of time. Very few philosophers have followed him all the way to this conclusion.[6] Instead, by endorsing different elements of his argument, they generated two very different theories of the nature of time. McTaggart began by distinguishing two ways in which we conceptualise the ordering of events in time. First, every event is located somewhere in the past, present or future. When we think about this ordering of events, we also recognise that it is a fluid, changing ordering in one respect. It is not that events change their relative positions in this ordering. Instead, they maintain their relations to each other, but events that are now present will become past, while events that are now future will become present. My present typing will soon be past, and my future coffee break will become present. McTaggart called this ordering of events 'the A-series'.

Second, every event stands in some temporal relation to every other event. The event of my typing is earlier than the event of my coffee break. This ordering of events is not fluid and dynamic like the A-series. The temporal relation that obtains between the events of my typing and my coffee break is fixed and unchanging. Furthermore, once we have fixed all events in terms of their temporal relations to each other, this ordering will be silent as to which of those events are happening now. Thus, this fixed ordering of times underdetermines any further distribution of events into the past, present and future. McTaggart called this ordering of events 'the B-series'.

To distinguish between the A-series and the B-series is merely to make an uncontroversial claim about the ways in which we observers represent the temporal locations and ordering of events in time. The very same events and moments can be ordered in these two different ways. The entire temporal history of the universe can be ordered as either an A-series or a B-series. We can think about the formation of the planets in our solar system as lying in the

---

[6] An exception is Sprigge (1992). See also Monton (2010) for a comparison between McTaggart's view of the unreality of time and the view in modern physics that there is no time at the fundamental level.

very distant past, or as earlier than the evolution of Homo sapiens. We can think about the death of our sun as lying in the distant future or as later than the COVID-19 pandemic of the early twenty-first century. Uncontroversial as this distinction is, genuinely substantial metaphysical questions arise as a result of drawing it: is one of these two ways of representing the temporal ordering of events more fundamental than the other? Does one of them truly represent the nature of time? Does a B-series ordering of events leave out an important feature of temporal reality, namely, an objective present moment?

Having drawn this distinction between the A-series and the B-series, McTaggart proceeds to set out his argument for the unreality of time. He first argues that the A-series is essential to time, so if events did not constitute an A-series, there would be no time. His reason for thinking this was that he thought, as many before him have thought, that change was essential for time and that unless time was constituted by an A-series, change would be impossible. A natural conclusion to draw at this point would be that time exists and is essentially constituted by an A-series. But McTaggart does not stop there. He goes on to argue that the notion of the A-series is self-contradictory, so it cannot be part of reality. According to McTaggart, the A-series must exist if there is to be time, but it cannot exist because it harbours a contradiction. It follows that time itself does not exist. I'll examine each element of McTaggart's argument in turn.

3.1.1 McTaggart's Thesis that the A-Series Is Essential to Time

McTaggart thinks that change is of the essence of time. There is a sense in which we all think this since we all think that time is the dimension of change. Change occurs when something possesses incompatible properties at different times: the petals of a rosebud are tightly packed, then open out and then fall away. But McTaggart means something more than this. For him, time *itself* exhibits change. Times, and the events that occur at them, change from being future to being present to being past. When McTaggart claims that time is the dimension of change, he means that it is the dimension of A-series change.

For McTaggart, the B-series relations of *earlier than* and *later than* are insufficiently temporal to constitute time. He ultimately thought that reality couldn't constitute a B-series without also constituting an A-series (McTaggart, 1927: §307–12). If events stood only in B-series relations, reality would consist of a set of entities standing permanently in transitive and asymmetric relations to each other, but those relations would not deserve to be called temporal relations because they are not associated with any kind of change (Ingthorsson, 2016: 35). The ordering of events relative to each other so that they constitute a B-series generates a fixed and unchanging ordering. Nothing about the B-series ever changes. This led McTaggart to conclude that a B-series that did not also constitute an A-series would not be a temporal series at all.

One way of thinking about the issue that McTaggart is grappling with here is in terms of the tension between being and becoming. If events are laid out in a B-series, standing in relations of *earlier than* and *later than* to each other, then there is a sense in which they all exist. They don't all exist *now*, of course, but they nevertheless exist – they exist *tenselessly*. But if all events exist tenselessly, how can they come to be and pass away? If one thinks that coming to be and passing away are essential to time, then one will find the B-series insufficient to adequately characterise it. If there is only a B-series so that all events are equally real, no matter when they occur, and no event ever changes its B-series location, then nothing really changes. Reality is a fixed and unchanging entity. In so far as there is a conflict between being and becoming, McTaggart, like Heraclitus, thought that becoming is essential to time. Mere being is insufficiently temporal.

McTaggart argued that change is essential to time, but change is not possible if time is constituted merely by a B-series. The possibility of change requires an A-series. An initial objection is that McTaggart assumes that change *just is* A-series change, so he begs the question (Dyke, 2002). It should not be surprising that there can be no A-series change unless time is constituted by an A-series. But why should we accept that assumption? Is there no acceptable B-series account of change?

McTaggart's opponents have long argued that there is an acceptable B-series account of change. His mistake, they argue, was to assume that the proper subjects of change are events, but it is not events that undergo change, it is objects (Russell, 1938; Smart, 1949; Mellor, 1981, 1998; Oaklander, 1984; Le Poidevin, 1991; Dyke, 2002). The event of the opening of the rosebud does not undergo change. Instead, the opening of the rosebud *is* a change: a change in the rosebud. McTaggart considered this objection, but took the view that any B-series account of change is insufficiently dynamic to constitute real change. He considers a poker that is hot at one time and cool at a later time but notes that nothing about those facts ever changes. Here again, it is hard not to see McTaggart as begging the question. Why should those facts themselves change in order for them to constitute a change?

McTaggart challenges a proponent of B-series change to point to a difference between the poker that is hot at one time and cool at a later time, and a poker that is hot at one end and cool at the other. The challenge is to differentiate B-series change from mere spatial variation. A poker's being hot at one end and cool at the other is mere variation of its properties along a spatial dimension. This does not count as change. Why, then, should variation of the poker's properties along the temporal dimension count as change? A proponent of B-series change could respond that variation in an object's properties along the temporal dimension counts as change precisely because time, and not space, is the dimension of change. But this response is as question-begging as McTaggart's own. A better response is that the temporal dimension differs from any spatial dimension in that causation operates along the temporal dimension, but not along any spatial dimensions (Mellor, 2013: 180). Changes occur because they are caused to happen by prior events and states of affairs (Mellor, 2013: 178). The proponent of B-series change can point to a relevant difference between the temporal dimension and any spatial dimension, which qualifies the temporal dimension as the dimension of change.

Proponents of A-series change, like McTaggart, argue that real change requires that the sum total of temporal facts changes over time (Leininger, 2021: 5). The division of events into past, present and future is transient and ever-changing. One who opposes the view that A-series change is real cannot accept this account of change. But it does not follow, as McTaggart argued, that she thereby rejects the reality of change itself. Instead, she can offer an alternative account of the nature of change. The dispute will then turn on what is the correct account of change, but McTaggart's argument that without an A-series there can be no time has been effectively undermined.

Ultimately, McTaggart's argument that change requires the A-series rests on a particular understanding of the notion of change. Change, for McTaggart, is the robust passage of events from future to present to past; it is A-series change. But then, his argument need not overly concern a proponent of B-series change. It establishes nothing more than that without an A-series there cannot be A-series change. The conclusion is a conditional: if there is an A-series, then there is A-series change. A proponent of B-series change can accept this conditional; it is true because both antecedent and consequent are false. If the existence of time depends on the existence of A-series change, then it would indeed follow that without an A-series there could not be time. But all McTaggart has established is that the existence of the A-series depends on the existence of A-series change.

3.1.2 McTaggart's Thesis that the A-Series is Contradictory

Much scholarly ink has been spilt about this element of McTaggart's argument. Some have dismissed it as a terrible argument (Broad, 1938; Christensen, 1974; Zimmerman, 2005). Others take it more seriously but disagree over whether it succeeds. I will present the argument in McTaggart's terms, and then offer an alternative presentation of it that I think better demonstrates the contradiction McTaggart identified.

The argument is both deceptively simple and strangely uncompelling. The first premise is that the A-series positions are incompatible with each other. Nothing can be both past and present, or both present and future. These A-determinations are mutually exclusive; each event can possess only one. But the second premise states that every event occupies every A-series position. Every event lies in the past, the present and the future. It follows that every event both *is* and *is not* past, present and future, which is a contradiction. The obvious response is to reject the second premise. No event is past, present and future *at the same time*, but only successively, and there is no contradiction in anything satisfying incompatible predicates at different times. Indeed, that is just what change *is*. So, an event *is* present, *will be* past and *has been* future.

McTaggart considers and rejects this response. He asks, 'But what is meant by "has been" and "will be"?' (McTaggart, 1927: 21). We mean, says McTaggart, that an event is present at a moment of present time, past at some moment of future time and future at some moment of past time. But every moment of time, as well as every event, is past, present and future, and so the problem arises again. McTaggart goes on: 'If M [an event] is present, there is no moment of past time at which it is past. But the moments of future time, in which it is past, are equally moments of past time, in which it cannot be past' (McTaggart, 1927: 21). It's easy to see why many have thrown up their hands in exasperation at McTaggart's presentation of the argument!

But is there a contradiction lurking in the notion of the A-series? I believe there is, and an alternative expression of McTaggart's objection will make it clear. To hold that the A-series is real or, to put it another way, to hold that tense is a feature of objective temporal reality, is to commit to two claims. These are, first, that there is an objective distinction between past, present and future that is not merely dependent on the temporal perspective of any given observer. If there were no observers there would still be an objective fact about which events are past, present, and future. The second claim is that events undergo continual change in their A-determinations. The reality of tense involves the reality of the passage of time. A past event was not always past; it was once present. A future event will not always be future; it will become present and then past.

It is worth noting that these two claims are variants of the two central elements of our folk theory of time. In my view, commitment to both of these claims is an essential feature of the notion of tense or the A-series. That is, one cannot commit to one without committing to the other. Suppose, for a moment, that there is an objective distinction between past, present and future but no passage of time. This would yield a static 'snap-shot' picture of time, with every event and moment stuck in just one A-series location. The events that are present are only ever present. My present typing is only ever present, and my future coffee break is only ever future. Surely, this is simply a false account of temporal reality, refuted by our ordinary experience. Now consider the alternative: could there be temporal passage if there were no distinction between past, present and future? As long as passage is conceived as a change in which events are present, or the change that events undergo from future to present to past,[7] committing to the reality of passage requires a commitment to the objective distinction between past, present and future.

The two component claims of asserting the reality of tense, or the A-series, are thus both essential to that assertion. But they are also (and this, I believe, is essentially McTaggart's objection) incompatible with each other. Time cannot be such that there is *both* a distinction between past, present and future *and* robust temporal passage (Dyke, 2001). The distinction between past, present and future can only be maintained if temporal passage is omitted from the picture. Any attempt to incorporate temporal passage into the picture results in the collapse of that distinction. To see this, consider again the supposition that there is an objective distinction between past, present and future, but no passage of time. According to this static, frozen picture of time, every event is fixed in one A-series location. But this picture is false, or at least, is only accurate for a moment. In order to rectify that we have to introduce the other component claim of the reality of tense: temporal passage. Different distributions of pastness, presentness and futurity obtain at different times. But as soon as we acknowledge that, we must recognise that every event occupies every A-series position, so the distinction between past, present and future collapses.

The contradiction at the heart of the A-series, then, is this. An objective distinction between past, present and future can only be drawn *at* some moment of time. But this yields a static, frozen picture of tensed time, a picture that is only accurate for a moment. To achieve a picture of temporal reality that is accurate for more than just a moment, we have to acknowledge that everything is constantly changing its A-series location. But acknowledging this involves recognising that everything successively occupies every A-series location. Thus, as soon as we try to incorporate temporal passage into the picture, we lose our ability to distinguish between past, present and future.

---

[7] This is what Skow (2015) refers to as 'robust passage'.

3.2 Alternative Accounts of the Tension at the Heart of the A-Series

We have already noted a fundamental tension between the ideas of temporal being and temporal becoming. If all events are temporally related to each other, how can they come to be and pass away? It's not hard to see the contradiction that McTaggart identified in the notion of the A-series as an alternative expression of this same tension. My articulation of this contradiction is another way of expressing this tension, and there have been many others.[8]

Price (2011), for example, describes it as attempting to combine two elements, which pull in opposite directions.[9] 'On the one hand, it wants to be *exclusive*, saying that one moment is objectively distinguished [as present]. On the other hand it wants to be *inclusive*, saying that all moments get their turn' (Price, 2011: 278). The urge to be exclusive drives the claim that there is an objective present moment, and thus that reality divides objectively into past, present and future. But this is an incomplete characterisation of tensed time, because if we stop there, attempting to do justice to exclusivity, we merely depict a frozen present moment (Price, 2011: 281). Hence, we must accommodate the urge to inclusivity, allowing that which moment is present undergoes change. But that move threatens to eliminate the exclusive element, because every moment is present.

Yet another way of articulating the tension is in terms of the two philosophical tendencies that I introduced in Section 1. The tendency to subject-relative understanding drives us to understand the world as it is from our distinctively human perspective. Seeking to satisfy this tendency, we incorporate our perspective on time, and our temporal experience, into our account of temporal reality. Thinking of time in this way generates an A-series, with temporal reality divided into past, present and future. But the tendency to subject-neutral understanding forces us to recognise that the temporal perspective we occupy right now will soon be replaced by a different temporal perspective, and then another and so on. We cannot just incorporate one perspective on time. We must recognise that there are as many temporal perspectives as there are times. But recognising that results in losing our grip on the distinctive nature of our present temporal perspective. It's just one of many temporal perspectives.

An alternative way of attempting to accommodate the tendency to subject-neutral understanding is to recognise that our perspective on temporal reality gives us a limited and partial view of it, so we ought to transcend it and adopt an objective,

---

[8] See for example, Mellor (1981, 1998), Oaklander (2004), Tallant (2010a) and Smith (2011).

[9] Price is specifically discussing the 'moving spotlight' view here, but I take his point about the tension between exclusivity and inclusivity to be common to any account that attempts to combine an objective distinction between past, present and future, and temporal passage.

atemporal perspective. This gives us a view of temporal reality that is from no particular temporal perspective, the 'Archimedean view of reality . . . the view from *nowhen*' (Price, 1996: 4) or 'God's eye view' (Williams, 1978; Nagel, 1989).[10] This approach leads us to think of how events are related to each other, and not how they are related to us, from our particular temporal point of view. Thinking of time in this way, therefore, generates a B-series. It also seems to completely abandon any attempt to account for the nature of time as it appears to us from our temporal perspective.

Another interpretation of McTaggart's argument is given by Fine (2005). He discerns within McTaggart's argument a commitment to four principles:

> *Realism* Reality is composed of tensed facts.
>
> *Neutrality* No time is privileged; the facts that compose reality are not oriented towards one time as opposed to another.
>
> *Absolutism* The composition of reality is not irreducibly relative, that is, its relative composition by the facts must be explained in terms of its absolute composition by the facts.
>
> *Coherence* Reality is not irreducibly incoherent, that is, its composition by incompatible facts must be explained in terms of its composition by compatible facts. (Fine, 2005: 13)[11]

Realism involves a commitment to the view that there are tensed facts; facts about the A-series locations of objects, events and times, which would be true if time is constituted by McTaggart's A-series. Neutrality is the claim that there is no privileged time, such that reality is constituted by just the tensed facts that obtain at that time. The idea here is akin to that intended by Price's notion of inclusivity. Every moment gets its turn at being objectively present. It's a mistake to single out just one moment as objectively present, because we then lose our grip on the fact that objective presentness changes from moment to moment. Absolutism is the claim that, in so far as we can give a temporally relative account of reality (i.e. an account that is true from the perspective of some particular time), the truth of that account is dependent on the truth of some absolute, non-relative account of reality. This principle captures the idea behind the subject-neutral tendency to understanding. It assumes that there is, in principle, an account of reality as it is in itself that is available to us. Lastly, Coherence is the view that any account of

---

[10] Ismael (2011) criticises the metaphor of a 'God's eye view', but argues that we can do without it: '[w]hat we really mean to contrast is the embedded view of time from the perspective of a particular perceptual encounter with the world, and a representation that is invariant under transformations between such perspectives'. (Ismael, 2011: 479)

[11] Fine gives two versions of these four principles that he labels 'simple' and 'sophisticated'. The differences between them need not concern us here. This is the sophisticated version.

reality must be free of contradictions. There cannot be incompatible facts. Commitment to this principle underlies McTaggart's argument that the A-series cannot exist because it contains contradictory elements.[12]

Fine argues that these four principles are incompatible and that this incompatibility is what lies at the heart of McTaggart's argument. If Realism is true, tensed facts exist absolutely, but the existence of a tensed fact is tied to a particular temporal perspective, which conflicts with Neutrality, according to which no time is privileged. If we attempt to accommodate Neutrality, such that reality is not oriented towards one time as opposed to another, then we will have to recognise that temporal reality will be constituted by different sets of incompatible facts that obtain at different times. By Absolutism these different sets of incompatible facts constitute reality absolutely and this conflicts with Coherence.

Fine outlines four different positions that arise from the rejection of each of the four principles: 'standard realism', 'anti-realism', 'external relativism' and 'fragmentalism'. The first two of these positions are roughly equivalent to the standard A-theory and B-theory, respectively. 'Standard realism' accepts Realism and rejects Neutrality. It holds that there are tensed facts and that the facts that compose reality are oriented towards one time, the present moment. 'Anti-realism' rejects Realism and accepts Neutrality. There are no tensed facts, only tenseless facts, and no temporal perspective is privileged over any other. For both standard realism and anti-realism, the remaining two principles, Absolutism and Coherence, are not directly argued for, but accepted as background assumptions (Deng, 2013a: 23).

The remaining two positions, external relativism and fragmentalism, are attempts to retain both Realism and Neutrality, by rejecting one of Absolutism and Coherence. Fine labels both these views 'non-standard realism'. Fragmentalism rejects Coherence, accepting that reality contains incompatible facts. External relativism rejects Absolutism, holding that tensed facts obtain relative to times. Deng (2013a) argues that neither constitutes a genuine alternative to the standard A-theory or B-theory. Fine himself admits that external relativism is 'a difficult, perhaps even an unintelligible, idea' (Fine, 2005: 403). Deng argues that it is a view that can, at best, only be gestured at. The way in which tensed facts exist relative to times on this view is not the tenseless, merely indexical, way in which every time is present relative to itself. Neither is it the standard A-theoretic way in which future times will be present, while past times were present. Instead, they are 'alternate realities'. They are not merely alternative perspectives on some more fundamental reality or

---

[12] We shall see in Section 3.3 that a way of retaining commitment to Coherence while also retaining something like the reality of the A-series is to reject the view that there can be a complete description of reality from no temporal perspective.

constituents of a bigger reality. 'In effect, [Fine's remarks about external relativism] amount to a kind of prohibition to search for un understanding of temporal reality in the usual ways' (Deng, 2013a: 28).

Attempting to make sense of fragmentalism is similarly fraught with difficulty. According to fragmentalism, incompatible facts compose reality *absolutely*, not merely relative to times, which would serve to alleviate the contradiction involved. Fine suggests that the facts 'arrange themselves' into coherent fragments (Fine, 2006: 402). But what keeps these coherent fragments out of each other's hair, so as to avoid contradiction? As Deng argues, 'Whenever it seems intelligible, it is very likely being mistaken for the B-theoretic view that temporally relativised (i.e. tenseless) facts from all times obtain equally' (Deng, 2013a: 28). Ultimately, neither version of non-standard realism succeeds in avoiding the contradiction at the heart of the A-series[13] or as Deng puts it,

> [N]on-standard realism does not constitute a genuine alternative. It is the conceptual gesture that results from trying to do full justice to our intuitive picture of passage. That picture is composed of incompatible elements which together deprive it of literal content. (Deng, 2013a: 29)

3.3 Dummett's McTaggart

One final interpretation of the contradiction at the heart of the A-series derives from Michael Dummett's (1960) defence of McTaggart. Dummett argues that what McTaggart's argument really shows is that there cannot be a complete description of reality independent of some temporal perspective. His interpretation thus goes to the heart of the tension that I have identified between the two philosophical tendencies. He wants to push back against the subject-neutral tendency to give an account of the nature of reality that transcends any particular point of view.

Dummett argues that McTaggart assumes that there *can* be a complete description of reality independent of some temporal perspective. When that assumption is combined with the view that time essentially involves the A-series, the contradiction quickly follows: if time is real, the complete description of reality contains incompatible elements, namely, for any event *e*, *e* is past, present *and* future. McTaggart concludes that, since the complete description of reality cannot contain incompatible elements, time is not real. Dummett concludes instead that we should reject the assumption that there can in principle be

---

[13] However, see Lipman (2015) for an attempt to revive fragmentalism as a viable view.

a complete description of reality. Time is real, but reality only contains *some* of the incompatible temporal facts, namely, a consistent subset of them.

So characterised, Dummett's view does not fit neatly into any of the four positions outlined by Fine, although it seems to be closer to non-standard realism than to either standard realism or anti-realism. However, it is far from clear that Dummett's view can be interpreted as either a rejection of Coherence or a rejection of Absolutism. Dummett clearly doesn't think that reality contains incompatible facts, as it is this prospect that prompts him to reject the view that there can be a complete description of reality. But neither does he reject the view that the composition of reality is absolute, as opposed to merely relative.

In his discussion of Dummett's argument, Falvey (2010) suggests that the notion of a complete description of reality that Dummett is here rejecting is the notion that Bernard Williams (1978) calls the 'absolute conception of reality', and Thomas Nagel (1989) calls 'the view from nowhere'. It is a notion associated with a particular understanding of the goal of metaphysical enquiry, which is to describe reality as it is in itself, setting aside any 'idiosyncratic conceptions of individuals differently situated or differently equipped cognitively' (Falvey, 2010: 300).

In order to achieve this goal, we need to strip away any elements of a description that arise as a result of an individual's particular perspective on reality, or the cognitive equipment with which she perceives or describes it. If we leave those elements in our description, it will inevitably include contradictory elements, because reality can be accurately described from more than one incompatible perspective or using different cognitive equipment. Hence, those contradictory elements will not reflect any underlying disagreement about the nature of reality (Falvey, 2010: 300). Tensed descriptions are paradigm examples of descriptions that incorporate elements of the temporal perspective of the person doing the describing. When I say, on Tuesday, 'It's raining', and my friend says, on Wednesday, 'It's not raining', we are not disagreeing. My judgement describes the weather in Dunedin on Tuesday, and my friend's judgement describes it in Dunedin on Wednesday. The complete description of reality needs to strip away these apparently conflicting judgements, to get to the underlying description of reality about which we do not disagree, namely, that it rains in Dunedin on Tuesday and it does not rain in Dunedin on Wednesday.

Other elements of our perspective on reality can similarly infect our judgements about it, such as facts about our perceptual and cognitive equipment. Take colour perception, for example. One view of the nature of colour is that it is a mind-independent phenomenon, such as a reflectance property of surfaces. Such views have difficulty accounting for the fact that different creatures with different visual systems, or similar creatures under different lighting conditions, can have different experiences in response to these

reflectance properties. An opposing view takes colour properties to be relations between objects and perceivers. Different creatures, with different
perceptual faculties and visual systems, might have different perceptual
experiences in response to the same object, and thus make conflicting judgements about that object's colour. Incorporating these different judgements
into a description of reality would result in a description with incompatible
components, but there need be no disagreement between such creatures about
the underlying nature of reality.

We need to find a way to express the fact that there is a single reality, on the
nature of which different perceivers do not disagree, but which we represent
differently due to our particular perspective on it and our particular cognitive
equipment. We do this by stepping back to form a conception of reality that
includes facts about the judgements, such as the time and place at which they are
made, and a characterisation of the perceptual and cognitive equipment of the
beings that make them. The absolute conception of reality is the limit that we
approach as we correct for more and more of the idiosyncrasies of the limited
and partial conceptions of reality that rational beings hold.

According to Falvey, the McTaggart–Dummett argument shows us that 'there
is no way of stating consistently and coherently all the tensed truths expressed
by speakers or thinkers differently situated in time, in terms that still retain some
measure of tensed content' (Falvey, 2010: 302). We can give a consistent tensed
description, but to do so, we must tie it to a particular temporal perspective. But
this is a limited and partial view of temporal reality. The absolute conception of
temporal reality must be a view not tied to any particular position in time. The
absolute conception of reality is a 'view from nowhen' (Falvey, 2010: 303),
a statement of the facts, including the facts of how individuals are situated with
respect to events, from no particular temporal point of view.

This discussion of the McTaggart–Dummett argument illustrates the import-
ance of getting our methodological approach right, as discussed in Section 2.
We saw there that there are many sources of information about the nature of
time, and part of the metaphysician's job is to marshal the information from
these different sources into a coherent, objective account. One such source of
information is the nature of our temporal experience. However, we need to be
wary of reading our metaphysics straight off our temporal experience, because
there are many possible explanations of that experience, only one of which is
that time really has the properties attributed to it by our folk theory. We may be
in a comparable position with respect to time that we are in with respect to
colour properties. That is, our temporal perspective, combined with our perceptual and cognitive apparatus, may incline us to draw conclusions about the
nature of time that are only true 'for us'. We ought to try to approach the

absolute conception of temporal reality by correcting for the idiosyncrasies of our limited, partial and peculiarly human, perspective on it.

3.4 Conclusion

McTaggart reached his conclusion by arguing that if time exists it must constitute an A-series and that it cannot do so, because there is a contradiction embedded within the notion of the A-series. Almost no one follows McTaggart all the way to his conclusion that time is unreal. Instead, the two theses for which he argues on the way to that conclusion have divided philosophers into two broad camps. Those who endorse his first, positive, thesis, that time essentially involves an A-series, have come to be known as A-theorists. A-theorists reject McTaggart's second, negative, thesis, that the notion of the A-series is contradictory. In the other camp, B-theorists endorse McTaggart's negative thesis but reject his positive thesis. They hold that time is real, and is constituted by a B-series, with events and times standing in temporal relations to each other, but there is no objective present, and no flow of time.[14]

A third response to McTaggart's argument, as we saw from the discussion of Dummett's defence of it, is to reject the assumption that there can be a complete description of reality from no temporal point of view. One way of interpreting Dummett here is as accepting McTaggart's positive thesis that the A-series is essential to time, and rejecting his negative thesis, that the A-series is self-contradictory. He does this by rejecting the assumption that every temporal perspective needs to be accommodated when giving an account of the objective nature of temporal reality. If we only need to accommodate one temporal perspective, then each moment and each event only occupies one A-series location, so the contradiction is avoided. Understood in this way, Dummett's response is better characterised as resulting in an A-theory. However, it is a static, frozen, A-series as, by privileging one temporal perspective, he is unable to incorporate A-series change into the account.

Having shown how the two broad approaches to the metaphysics of time[15] emerged out of McTaggart's argument, I turn now to examine those two approaches in more depth.

---

[14] Different labels have also been applied to the two camps in this debate. A-theorists are also known as dynamic theorists, tensed theorists and tensers. B-theorists are also known as static theorists, tenseless theorists and detensers. While acknowledging that the labels derived from McTaggart's argument are not the most illustrative of the available options, for simplicity's sake I will stick with them.

[15] There is also a third approach to the metaphysics of time that emerges out of McTaggart's work, known as the C-theory. McTaggart discussed a C-series in addition to an A- and a B-series. The C-series differs from the B-series in that it lacks an intrinsic direction. The C-theory is defended in Farr (2020a). I will set aside discussion of the C-theory to focus on the two principal theories.

4 The A-Theory

The term 'A-theory' really refers to a cluster of theories that differ in significant ways. One point of difference is that they recognise the existence of different elements of a tensed reality. Some recognise the existence of past, present and future, while events and times undergo change in the A-series properties they possess. Others recognise the existence of just the past and the present; the future being non-existent. Others take just the present moment to exist. But it's perhaps more helpful at this point to focus on what they all have in common. They all agree that there is an objectively distinguished present moment and that time is dynamic, but they have different ways of cashing out these two central claims. Thus, they take the two features that I identified in Section 2 as essential to our folk theory of time, to be genuine features of the nature of time. I will outline some of these variants of the A-theory.

4.1 Ontological Variants of the A-Theory

The 'moving spotlight' theory (Cameron, 2015) takes all moments, objects and events, whether they be past, present or future, to exist. But the present moment is distinguished from all the rest by being 'illuminated' by the spotlight of the present. Talk of a spotlight here must, of course, be metaphorical. Nevertheless, the view can be understood as recognising the existence of events and moments constituting a B-series, but adding to that view a distinguished present moment that divides events into past, present and future. An early, and still influential, account of this view was given by Broad (1923):

> We are naturally tempted to regard the history of the world as existing eternally in a certain order of events. Along this, and in a fixed direction, we imagine the characteristic of presentness as moving, somewhat like the spot of light from a policeman's bulls-eye traversing the fronts of houses in a street. (Broad, 1923: 67)

Presentness, on this view, is an objective feature of reality that cannot be reduced to mere simultaneity between an event and an observer. A description of temporal reality that detailed just the temporal relations in which events and times stand to each other (i.e. a B-series) would lack some crucial information, namely, which of those times is present. If there were no observers, there would still be a present moment, and which moment that is would be continually changing. This view accounts for the dynamic nature of time in terms of the continual change in which moment is objectively distinguished as present by the metaphorical moving spotlight.

A variant of this theory is one that accounts for the dynamic nature of time in terms of objects, events and moments acquiring and losing A-properties of pastness, presentness and futurity. Just as with the moving spotlight view, every moment exists, but they are differentiated in terms of their possession of A-properties, and they continually undergo change in that respect. So, for example, Queen Elizabeth I has the property of pastness, the COVID-19 pandemic of the early twenty-first century has the property of presentness and the year 2500 has the property of futurity. There are also finer gradations of these properties, such that an event might have the property of being 51 minutes past, which it loses to acquire the property of being 52 minutes past, and so on.

The 'growing block' theory acknowledges the existence of past and present moments, objects and events, but takes the future to be non-existent (Tooley, 1997; Forrest, 2004; Forbes, 2016; Correia & Rosenkranz, 2018). What distinguishes the present moment on this view is that there is nothing to which it stands in the *earlier than* relation. It occupies a position at the 'cutting edge' of reality. The view was vividly described by Broad as a theory that

> [a]ccepts the reality of the present and the past, but holds that the future is simply nothing at all. Nothing has happened to the present by becoming past except that fresh slices of existence have been added to the total history of the world. (Broad, 1923: 66–67)

The growing block view accounts for the dynamic nature of time in terms of the continual addition of new present moments (fresh slices of existence!) to the already existing block of past moments and the most recent present moment. As Broad puts it 'the sum total of existence is always increasing' (Broad, 1923: 72) and it is this change, or increase, in what exists that gives time its dynamic character.

Presentism is a theory that acknowledges the existence of just one moment, the present moment (Markosian, 2004; Zimmerman, 2005, 2008; Bourne, 2006). Reality is exhausted by everything that presently exists. Prior described it well when he said that '[t]he present simply is the real considered in relation to two particular species of unreality, namely, the past and the future'. (Prior, 1970: 245) It should be clear that what distinguishes the present moment on this view is simply that it consists of all that exists, in contrast with the non-existent past and future. But how does this view account for the dynamic nature of time? According to presentists, the sum total of existence, all that is present, is continually changing. So the dynamic nature of time consists in a change in what exists.

Presentism is often contrasted with eternalism, the view that all times, and their contents are equally real. Eternalism can be seen as the ontological component of the B-theory, but a distinctive debate has developed between presentism and eternalism, *qua* theories of temporal ontology, as a sub-genre of the debate between the A-theory and the B-theory.[16] Some have responded to this debate by arguing that the debate between presentism and eternalism lacks substance; that far from being opposing views about temporal ontology, they are merely notational variants of one another.[17] This debate has evolved into yet another sub-genre of the debate between the A-theory and the B-theory. Trivialists argue that eternalists and presentists mean different things by 'exists', so that when the presentist says 'Only present things exist' and the eternalist says 'Non-present things exist', they are not disagreeing.

Much has been written over the last century both in support of, and against, each of these variants of the A-theory, both by those opposed to the A-theory in general (B-theorists), and those defending particular variants of the A-theory, giving the debate a rather complex dialectic. Defenders of one A-theoretic variant argue that their view is superior to other A-theoretic variants in various ways, or that their view is immune to problems facing other variants of the A-theory. A growing block theorist, for example, may endorse a B-theorist's argument against presentism, while also rejecting the B-theorist's view overall. Rather than enter the complex fray between competing variants of the A-theory, my focus will be on what can be said both for and against the A-theoretic approach in general.

4.2 Reasons in Support of the A-Theory

The two essential elements to any A-theory of time are the claims that the present moment is objectively distinguished and that time is dynamic. These two claims are also the essential elements of our folk theory of time, which is based on our temporal experience. Proponents of the A-theory thus prioritise the philosophical tendency to subject-relative understanding of the world as it appears to us. The first thing to say in support of the A-theory, then, is that, prima facie, it fits with our ordinary temporal experience. We could go further, as many have (Gale, 1968; Schuster, 1986; Schlesinger, 1991, 1994; Smith, 1994; Craig, 2000), and argue that our ordinary temporal experience gives us reason to think that the A-theory is true. That is, we could construct an argument *from* the nature of temporal experience *to* the A-theory. Such an argument might go something like this:

---

[16] See, for example, Crisp (2003), Rea (2003), Markosian (2004) and Miller (2013).

[17] Lombard (1999), Callender (2000, 2011), Meyer (2005), Savitt (2006) and Dorato (2006a) argue in favour of the triviality thesis. Hinchliff (1996, 2000), Sider (1999, 2001, 2006), Crisp (2004) and Markosian (2004) argue against it.

The Argument from Temporal Experience

1. We have experiences as of an objectively distinguished present moment and as of temporal passage.[18]
2. If we have experiences as of an objectively distinguished present moment, and as of temporal passage, then any reasonable explanation of this relies on an objectively distinguished present moment and temporal passage being objective features of reality.
3. Therefore, an objectively distinguished present moment and temporal passage are objective features of reality.

We will explore this argument, and possible responses to it, in greater depth in Section 6. For now, it suffices to note that something like this argument may represent at least part of the thinking that underlies support for the A-theory.

As well as being, prima facie, a better fit with our temporal experience, the A-theory also looks like a better fit with ordinary, commonsense beliefs about time. The fact that it bears such a strong resemblance to our folk theory of time is testament to that fact. Recall the goal of metaphysical enquiry, which is to provide an account of some feature of reality that is objectively true. One common starting point for such investigations, particularly among empiricist philosophers, is our commonsense beliefs about that feature of reality.[19] This does not mean that commonsense beliefs about reality cannot be defeated, but there is a general heuristic that it is better, in a metaphysical theory, to avoid denying widely and strongly held beliefs if at all possible. The A-theoretic approach thus, arguably, has common sense, intuition and experience on its side.[20] Of course, common sense, intuition and experience have all been shown to be wrong about some features of reality. Nevertheless, the A-theory seems to occupy the default position with respect to the nature of time, with the burden of proof falling squarely on the shoulders of those who oppose it.[21]

4.3 Objections to the A-Theory

We have already spent some time discussing the two principal objections to the A-theory. The first is the apparent contradiction that lies at the heart of the A-series. According to McTaggart and his followers in this regard, time cannot

---

[18] Talk of experiences 'as of' an objectively present moment and temporal passage signals that this claim is neutral as to whether or not these experiences are veridical.

[19] The 'Canberra Plan' is a philosophical methodology that takes commonsense beliefs or 'platitudes' as a starting point (Jackson, 1998).

[20] Although, see Forbes (2015) who argues that facts about temporal topology cannot account for this experience, and also Prosser (2016) who argues that we *couldn't* detect temporal passage, even if it existed.

[21] However, see Dyke (2011) for an argument that the burden of proof falls more evenly on A-theorists and B-theorists than this suggests.

be such that there is an objective present moment *and* temporal passage. The second objection is the A-theory's prima facie incompatibility with STR. It seems that the deliverances of both logic and science undermine the A-theory. I turn now to look at some further objections to the A-theory.

4.3.1 The 'Two Times' Objection

The 'two times' objection arises out of attempts to give a coherent account of temporal passage.[22] What is it for time to flow, or for temporal passage to be a real phenomenon? When we say that time flows, we seem to be saying that events are continually changing their position in relation to the present moment, or that we, occupying the present, are steadily advancing towards the future. This description is, to some extent, metaphorical (Williams, 1951: 460). The metaphor suggests something like the feeling you get when you are sitting in a train watching the countryside whizzing past you. On this picture, the train represents the present moment, and the countryside beyond the train represents the events going on in the world spread out in time. Those that are parallel with you are present, those that you have already passed are in the past and those that you haven't yet reached are in the future. But the description can only be metaphorical as, unlike the train, the present does not move from place to place.

So what does the supposed movement of the present consist in? Let's examine the comparison with ordinary movement a little more closely. What does the ordinary movement of an object consist in? We say that an object has moved when it is located at one place at one time and at a different place at a later time. So ordinary movement is change in spatial location relative to change in temporal location. But if temporal passage consists in the movement of the present, and we are to understand this movement in the same way, then the present must occupy one *time* at one time and a *different* time at a later time! This account either makes no sense, or it requires us to introduce a further temporal dimension relative to which the movement of the present takes place. The movement of the present seems to be a process that takes time to happen, and in order for that to be the case, there needs to be a second temporal dimension relative to which the movement of the present along the ordinary temporal dimension takes place.

Now, suppose the A-theorist accepts that the movement of the present requires a second temporal dimension. Call it 'hyper-time'. What should she say of this second temporal dimension? According to the A-theorist, two features are essential to time: an objective present moment and a dynamic nature. It follows that if hyper-time is genuinely temporal, it must have an objective present moment

---

[22] An early statement of this objection is given in Broad (1938). Schlesinger (1982) attempts to rebut it. See MacBeath (1986) for a critique of Schlesinger.

and a dynamic nature. But then, by the same reasoning, the movement of the present in hyper-time requires a third temporal dimension (hyper-hyper-time) relative to which it moves. And so we set off on an infinite regress. But even without the infinite regress, the notion of hyper-time is, arguably, an ad hoc notion, introduced solely to accommodate the postulation of a moving present. The notion does not appear in any scientific theories about time, and it does no further explanatory work. By Ockham's Razor, we ought not to postulate it.

The A-theorist could attempt to block the infinite regress by arguing that the present moment in ordinary time moves relative to hyper-time, while the present moment in hyper-time moves relative to ordinary time. But even if successful in stopping the regress, this move generates a two-dimensional picture of time, and what evidence do we have for that? Ordinary experience certainly does not support such a picture. It's an empirical question whether there is any scientific evidence to support this view. An initial survey of scientific thinking about time does not look promising. Given that ordinary experience and commonsense thinking about time are supposed to support the A-theory, it is problematic, to say the least, that following this line of thought leads us to a view for which there appears to be little, if any, empirical support.

4.3.2 The 'Rate of Passage' Objection

The 'rate of passage' objection arises when we follow another attempt to make sense of temporal passage. If the present really moves through time (setting aside worries generated by the 'two times' objection), then it moves through time at a certain rate. But a rate is a change in one dimension relative to a change in another dimension. 'Kilometres per hour' is a rate of change along a spatial dimension, measured in kilometres, relative to change along the temporal dimension, measured in hours. If a car moves, it makes sense to ask at what rate it moves. How many kilometres will it travel in an hour? But it's not clear that it makes sense to ask how fast the present moves along the temporal dimension.

What sort of answer should we expect to this question? One second per second? But one second per second is not a rate (Olson, 2009), just as one kilometre per kilometre is not a rate. The objection can be developed in two ways. The first is to argue that if the present really moves, there should be a rate at which it moves, but there is no such rate, so the present does not really move. Any motion, whatever it is motion of, requires a rate at which it occurs. The only possible answer to the question of how fast time flows is one second per second, but that is not a rate, so there is no rate at which the present moves.[23]

---

[23] For discussion of this objection see Olson (2009), Phillips (2009), Tallant (2010b, 2016), Raven (2011) and Skow (2011a).

The second way of developing the objection introduces the notion of hyper-time again. If there is a rate at which time flows, there must be a further temporal dimension, because a rate is, by definition, a change in one dimension relative to a change in another dimension. In order for one second per second to count as a genuine rate of change, we need two temporal dimensions, so that the present moves at a rate of one second of ordinary time for every second of hyper-time, for example. But as we've seen, introducing hyper-time violates Ockham's razor, is ad hoc, we can't observe it and science hasn't detected it, so there is no good reason to believe that it exists.

Set aside these worries about hyper-time for a moment and suppose that there *is* a rate at which time flows. Could that rate change? Could time speed up or slow down?[24] Whatever the rate is, it's logically possible that it could be faster or slower. What if it changed? Would we be able to detect such a change? The suggestion that the rate at which time passes could speed up or slow down, and that this would be undetectable, threatens this account with incoherence.[25]

While they have been challenged,[26] the 'two times' and 'rate of passage' objections suggest that attempts to make sense of the powerful and intuitive idea that time is dynamic do not withstand critical scrutiny. What has gone wrong? One answer is, as Williams (1951: 463) put it, that true motion is motion in time *and* space. Nothing can move just in time, in the same way that nothing can move just in space. The concepts that we employ when we attempt to capture the notion of temporal passage, such as, for example, the concepts of movement, change, flow, approaching, receding and so on, are all *temporal* concepts. That is, they all presuppose the existence of a temporal dimension against which they take place. So, when we apply them to time itself, we inevitably require a further temporal dimension in order to make sense of this application. Stating the intuitive belief that time flows involves applying these already temporal concepts to time itself. Taking these intuitive metaphors seriously lands us in conceptual confusion.

4.3.3 Fine's Objection: The A-Theory Is Just as Static as the B-Theory

According to this objection, despite appearances, and claims to the contrary, the A-theory is unable to accommodate temporal passage. Recall Fine's (2005)

---

[24] See Dyke, H. (2020). *Our experience of time in the time of coronavirus*, www.cambridgeblog.org /2020/05/our-experience-of-time-in-the-time-of-coronavirus-lockdown/ for a B-theoretic explanation of the phenomenon whereby, under certain conditions, time *appears* to speed up or slow down.

[25] However, see Miller and Norton (2021) for an argument that time could pass at different rates in different sub-regions of a world.

[26] See, for example, Phillips (2009).

'standard realism', essentially the A-theory. Fine asks how the standard realist can account for the passage of time. The standard realist has the resources to account for one moment being objectively present, and therefore also for all other moments occupying some other position in the A-series. She can say, for example, that presentness is a 'genuinely absolute and objective feature of things' (Fine, 2005: 287). She can also 'maintain that the present time t (and any other present thing) is present' (Fine, 2005: 287). But, Fine argues, this does nothing to help her account for the passage of time. The passage of time requires that different moments of time be successively present. And this 'appears to require more than the presentness of a single moment of time' (Fine, 2005: 287).

It will not help, Fine argues, for the standard realist to say that some other, future, time *will be* present, or some other, past, time *was* present. For this still merely describes how things are *now*. It locates all times somewhere in a static, unchanging A-series. The future presentness of some time, and the past presentness of some other time, amounts to no more than the present time's being present, while another time is later than the present, and yet another time is earlier than the present. Fine's objection to standard realism, then is this: it is ultimately equivalent to the anti-realist, or B-theoretic view, with the addition of a privileged centre. With its collection of tensed facts oriented towards one time, the present time, it designates an A-series location for every time. But the picture it so delivers is a frozen, static, A-series. The standard realist's conception of temporal reality, according to Fine, is 'as static, or block-like as the anti-realist's, the only difference lying in the fact that his block has a privileged centre' (Fine, 2005: 287).

Fine's criticism harks back to my interpretation of the apparent contradiction at the heart of the A-series, discussed in Section 3.1.2. I noted there that commitment to the reality of the A-series requires commitment to two claims: that there is an objective distinction between past, present and future and that everything continually changes its A-series location. The problem is that it is not possible to commit to both of these claims. Accepting an objective distinction between past, present and future, yields a static, frozen A-series. Fine's criticism is that the standard realist can get only this far, but the position so arrived at is false. As we saw, attempting to incorporate A-series change leads to an inevitable relinquishing of the distinction between past, present and future, because every moment occupies every A-series location as a result of undergoing A-series change.

Deng (2013a) agrees with Fine that standard realism fails to capture the dynamic nature of time, and as a consequence, is far less dynamic an account than it is ordinarily taken to be. Even granting standard realism the claim that different times are metaphysically privileged in the way that the present moment is now privileged, it still lacks the conceptual resources to explain how the metaphysical privilege of presentness passes from one moment to the next. She writes,

> [s]tandard realism really amounts to a multitude of different views, each privileging a different time. Each of its versions implies that certain times will be present and other times were. The reason this is not quite satisfactory is that the passage of time manifests itself more in a change between descriptions of temporal reality, than in the content of the descriptions themselves. (Deng, 2013a: 26)

Thus, standard realism either constitutes one frozen tensed description of temporal reality, or a multitude of different frozen tensed descriptions, but in the latter case it lacks the resources to explain how temporal reality undergoes change from being accurately depicted by one such description to being accurately depicted by another.

Boccardi (2015) takes an alternative route to essentially the same conclusion. He argues that McTaggart's 'no change' objection to the B-theoretic account of change can be generalised so that it also applies to A-theoretic accounts of time. He takes the target of this objection to be any comparative account of change, according to which we look at what is true at t_1 and what is true at t_2, and compare them. If they differ, there is change. If they do not differ, there is no change. But if the objection applies to any comparative account of change, it applies whether that account is given in tensed or tenseless terms. Thus, being realist about tense is not sufficient to express the fact that we live in a dynamic world (Boccardi, 2015: 172).

Dynamicists, who believe that things change only if reality itself changes, argue that a comparative account of change is not sufficient to account for genuine change. Change must be more than just having different properties at different times. It is a difference in what exists. But, argues Boccardi, an A-theoretic account of passage such as this is no less comparative an account of change than the B-theorist's 'at-at' (Russell, 1938) account of ordinary change. It takes a tensed description of reality that is true at one time and compares it with a different tensed description of reality that is true at another time. Since they are different, there has been change. But if the 'no change' objection works in the case of the B-theorist's account of ordinary change, then it will work in the case of the A-theorist's account of passage.

Like Fine and Deng, Boccardi argues that merely designating a moment as present is not sufficient to introduce a dynamic element into a tensed metaphysical account of time. Tense realists must add an extra element to their picture of the world, over and above A-determinations, to guarantee a dynamic ontology.

But what kind of extra fact can make it true that the world is dynamic? The problem is that any number of changeless, albeit tensed, descriptions of reality cannot express the fact that reality is dynamic. A multitude of such descriptions cannot express the fact that the world changes from being accurately represented by one of these descriptions, to being accurately represented by another. What, indeed, could guarantee that the world changes from being represented by the description at t_1 to that at t_2, to that at t_3 and so on? What would rule out a change in the world from being represented by the description at t_1 to that at t_{53}, to that at t_7? According to Crisp, a presentist, 'it's a brute, contingent fact that the ... times come temporally ordered as they do' (Crisp, 2007: 132). It's hard to see that appealing to brute, contingent facts at this point is going to be at all explanatory.

4.4 The Presentist Attempt to Accommodate Temporal Passage

Presentism is the view that only what is present exists and that reality undergoes continual change in what exists. It is widely thought that presentism succeeds as a response to McTaggart's paradox (Prior, 1970; Bigelow, 1996; Hinchliff, 1996; Craig, 1998; Crisp, 2005).[27] In this section I will explore whether this is true, and whether presentism has the resources to account for temporal passage.

According to McTaggart, temporal reality cannot be constituted by an A-series because, as he put it, the A-determinations of pastness, presentness and futurity are mutually incompatible, yet every moment possesses them all. The presentist response to this argument is to block the contradiction, or the regress of explanations, by claiming that nothing possesses any incompatible A-determinations, because only what is present exists. There are only present things. There are no past or future things, so nothing ever possesses more than one A-determination. But how does this account manage to incorporate temporal passage? If reality consists of everything that presently exists, then we have a static account of what exists now. As Pooley (2013) puts it, 'A natural thought at this point is that something crucial is still missing from the model. In what sense does it capture the passage of time? Doesn't the model need continual updating?' (Pooley, 2013: 327). But continual updating would only generate different tensed descriptions of what exists at different times, and as we saw in the previous section, without a mechanism for getting from one of these descriptions to the next, a multitude of different tensed descriptions is as static as a single tensed description. So presentism, it seems, is as vulnerable to the objection that it cannot accommodate passage as the standard A-theory.

---

[27] However, see Oaklander (2010) and Tallant (2010a) for arguments for the contrary view.

According to Pooley, Prior's (1968) presentist account of temporal passage avoids this criticism. Prior discusses an event six years in his past, when he fell out of a punt.[28] How, Pooley asks, is the Priorean presentist to account for changes in pastness and futurity that events continually undergo and that are constitutive of time's passage? The answer, he suggests, can be given in terms of conjunctions of iterated tensed claims. One year ago, Prior's fall from a punt was five years in the past, but now it is no longer five years in the past. In one year's time Prior's fall from a punt will be seven years past, and so on. But is this sufficient to account for the passage of time? Pooley thinks it is, and offers two reflections to assuage any doubts.

First, he asks us to compare these tensed claims with the presentist's expression of ordinary change, such as my change in shape when I go from standing to sitting. For the presentist, this amounts to the fact that I was standing and I am now sitting. So, for the presentist, ordinary change involves conjunctions of tensed claims about what is the case and what was the case, in the same way that time's passage involves conjunctions of tensed claims about how past and future events are, were and will be. For Pooley, if the presentist's account of ordinary change is acceptable, then her account of temporal passage is too. I want to resist the idea that the presentist's account of ordinary change is acceptable so, a fortiori, her account of temporal passage is unacceptable too.

The presentist's account of ordinary change is captured by the conjunction of claims, such as that I was standing and I am now sitting. Certainly, this implies that I *have* changed, but it does not capture the change. It merely describes how things are now. Things are now such that I am sitting and that I was standing. This would be satisfied by a static, frozen description of how things are now from this temporal perspective. Similarly, the conjunction of iterated tensed claims about how far in the past Prior's falling out of a punt is now, was last year and will be next year, all describe how things are now with respect to the distribution of events through temporal reality. It would also be satisfied by a fixed and static tensed reality.

To see this, and setting aside, just for a moment, the presentist doctrine that only the present exists, suppose that temporal reality is constituted by a fixed, tensed distribution of times and events, such that one moment is privileged as present, and the rest fall into their respective A-series locations. Imagine, if you will, a representation of temporal reality laid out before you as if on an unrolled reel of film, with a marker indicating which time, or which frame, is present. If temporal reality were so constituted, the claim that I was standing and am now sitting is satisfied, as long as the present frame includes me sitting and an earlier

---

[28] Prior eschews talk of events in favour of talk of things. This point need not concern us here.

frame includes me standing. No actual change in the representation of temporal reality laid out before you need take place in order to accommodate it.

The same is true of the complex tensed description of the changes in pastness and futurity that events, like Prior's falling out of a punt, undergo. Think of our film reel representation of temporal reality again. In order to locate Prior's falling out of a punt, we first identify the present and then locate the moment six years in the past (six frames to the left). In order to accommodate the claim that one year ago Prior's falling out of a punt was five years in the past, we locate the moment one year in the past (one frame to the left), and then locate Prior's falling out of a punt five years earlier than (five frames to the left of) that moment. In order to accommodate the claim that in one year's time the event will be seven years past, we locate the moment one year in the future (one frame to the right), and then note that the event is seven years earlier than (seven frames to the left of) that point. Nothing about our film reel representation of temporal reality, with its privileged present moment, needs to change to accommodate these claims. Hence, it is as fixed and static as a B-theoretic account of temporal reality.

Now we reintroduce the presentist doctrine that only the present exists, in order to see whether the objection succeeds against presentism in particular. If we consider just the present frame, then we will have a presentist model of temporal reality. As regards ordinary change, the presentist wants to say that it is true in the present frame that I am sitting, and also (somehow) true in that frame that I was standing. The model therefore satisfies the claim that I was standing and am now sitting, even though nothing about it exhibits any change. As regards temporal passage, we get the same result. Even allowing that one can truly describe from within the model that other times will be present and yet other times were present, this does nothing to generate any actual dynamism. The model, so described, is entirely static. In order to incorporate that dynamism, the presentist needs to explain how reality changes from one moment to the next. But without the resources of other times on which to peg the successively changing metaphysical privilege of presentness, it's not at all clear that she can do this.

Presentists generally introduce substitute, or ersatz, entities to do duty for past and future times. For some it is abstract entities (Bourne, 2006), for others it is maximally consistent sets of propositions (Crisp, 2007). So our presentist model of temporal reality has an entity of one kind as the present moment and entities of different kinds as past and future moments. However, this gets us no further than our original film reel model. With this new model, we still don't need to change anything about it in order to accommodate the conjunctions of tensed claims that supposedly constitute ordinary change and temporal passage. Presentism too is as fixed and static as a B-theoretic account of temporal reality.

4.5 Conclusion

I examined some varieties of A-theory that differ chiefly in terms of their ontological commitments. I focused on their common claims, namely, that there is a privileged present moment and temporal passage. If it can be shown that no metaphysical account of the nature of time can have both of these features, or that any proposed such account fails to incorporate the elements of temporal reality that it claims to accommodate, then it will be found wanting. I argued that attempts to accommodate a privileged present moment and temporal passage inevitably succumb to some version of the 'two times' problem or the 'rate of passage' problem.

McTaggart's paradox essentially arises because it is not possible to accommodate both these elements of our intuitive picture of time into one coherent, and true, metaphysical picture. But my discussion of the inevitability of running into either the 'two times' problem or the 'rate of passage' problem shows that there is also a problem with the notion of temporal passage itself. My diagnosis of this problem is that the concepts that we employ when attempting to capture the notion of temporal passage, the concepts of movement, change, flow and so on, all presuppose the existence of a temporal dimension against which they take place. Applying them to time itself generates the need for either a further temporal dimension in order to make sense of this application, or a rate at which this temporal passage takes place.

I then considered and endorsed Fine's objection that any A-theory is ultimately as static as the B-theory is claimed to be. This objection also demonstrates a problem with any attempt to accommodate the notion of temporal passage. Stating of other times that they will be, or were, present, does not get us beyond our current, privileged present moment. We are only able to describe, albeit in terms of complex, iterated tensed claims, how things are now. That is a consistent account, but it is a static and unchanging one, so fails to accommodate temporal passage.

The A-theory is borne out of an attempt to satisfy the philosophical tendency to understand the world as it appears to us. The problems it faces illustrate what can go wrong when we attempt to build a metaphysical theory out of our intuitive beliefs and experience without acknowledging that some of our beliefs, and some features of our experience, might be the product of particular features of us, and the means by which we experience reality, rather than the objective nature of reality itself.

5 The B-Theory

There is not as much variety among B-theoretic views as there is among A-theoretic views. B-theorists may disagree on some details, but there is broad agreement among them about the nature of temporal reality. For B-theorists, there is no privileged present moment, no objective distinction between past, present and future and no temporal passage. Since no moment is objectively present, the privilege of presentness cannot pass from one moment to the next. But these are all negative claims. What positive claims does the B-theory make about temporal reality?

For B-theorists, time is broadly equivalent to McTaggart's B-series. What McTaggart's paradox establishes, according to B-theorists, is the unreality, not of time, but of tense. It's not possible for time to be constituted by an A-series, but since the A-series is not essential to time, time exists, and is constituted by a B-series. Events and times stand in the temporal relations of *earlier than*, *later than* and *simultaneous with*, to each other.

An implication of the B-theory's rejection of an objective distinction between past, present and future is that all times are equally real. The A-theorist recognises the present moment as metaphysically privileged and typically cashes this privilege out in ontological terms. The present is *more real* than the past or the future. For the moving spotlight theorist, the present is the moment picked out by the spotlight of presentness. For the presentist, it is all that exists. For the growing block theorist, it is the moment at the 'cutting edge' of reality. But if there is no distinction between past, present and future, then there are no grounds for distinguishing between times in terms of ontological status. No time is metaphysically privileged, so all times are ontologically on a par.

For the B-theory time is much more like space than we ordinarily think. Just as there is no place that is objectively *here*, there is no time that is objectively *now*. Just as there is no reason to pick out what is spatially proximate (here) as more real than what is spatially distant, there is no reason to pick out what is temporally proximate (now) as more real than what is temporally distant. The moons of Jupiter are just as real as Dunedin, even though Dunedin is here and Jupiter's moons are far away. Similarly, the Spanish flu pandemic of the early twentieth century is just as real as the COVID-19 pandemic of the early twenty-first century. The pandemic that comes after the COVID-19 pandemic is just as real as the other two, even though we do not, yet, know much about it. Furthermore, just as there is no flow of space from here to there, there is no flow of time from future to present to past. Time, on the B-theory, is usually taken to be static.

The analogous treatment of time and space in these respects illustrates the difference in priority assigned by the B-theorist to the two philosophical tendencies. Where the A-theory prioritises the subject-relative tendency to understand time as it appears to us, the B-theory prioritises the subject-neutral tendency to understand time as it is independently of us. Calling a place 'here' picks out a relational feature of that place, namely, the relation that it stands in to the person using the term 'here'. Our use of spatially indexical terms incorporates an element of our perspective on reality into our description of it. Nobody expects such terms to appear in an objective description of how things are independently of us and our perspective on the world. Describing events as past, present, future or now, is analogous, for the B-theorist, to describing places as here or over there. Like the spatial indexicals, these terms incorporate an element of our own temporal perspective into our description of reality. We shouldn't expect them to appear in an objective description of how things are that is independent of us and our perspective. From the fact that we describe reality in tensed terms, from a particular temporal perspective, it does not follow that reality itself is tensed.

For the B-theory time is simply a dimension, much like the three spatial dimensions. Indeed, it is one dimension of four-dimensional space-time. The universe has both temporal and spatial extension; it is spread out in time just as it is spread out in space. It has both spatial and temporal parts, as do the objects that exist within it.[29] The world-line of an object shows the spatiotemporal coordinates at which it exists. Objects do not move through time. Instead, they are spread out along the temporal dimension, just as they are spread out along the spatial dimensions.

5.1 Objection: The B-Theory Conflicts with Commonsense Beliefs about Time

The B-theory clearly departs radically from our commonsense beliefs about time.[30] We do not ordinarily take time to be static; we take it to be dynamic. We do not ordinarily take all times to be equally real. While we believe that distant places are just as real as the place we call here, we do not normally take distantly past and future times to be just as real as the present. We accept that no place is objectively here – that hereness is merely a relational, egocentric feature that we ascribe to places depending on our spatial location. But we do not think the same is true of when now is. Nowness, we think, is an absolute, objective feature that

---

[29] Whether or not the universe, and the objects within it, have temporal parts is one issue on which B-theorists do disagree. Heller (1992) argues that they do. Mellor (1998) argues that they do not. Sider (2001) and Hawley (2001) argue that, rather than being four-dimensional and made up of temporal parts, objects are made up of three-dimensional stages. This disagreement need not concern us here.

[30] Whether, and to what extent, the commonsense beliefs about time that I outline here are in fact held by the folk is a matter for empirical investigation. My aim is merely to allude to the 'broad brush' beliefs that have proved remarkably persistent among both philosophers and non-philosophers, and to note that, to the extent that these beliefs are held, they appear to conflict with what the B-theory tells us about time. See also footnote 3.

picks out one time uniquely, not simply a relational, egocentric feature that we ascribe to times depending on our temporal location. And we do not ordinarily take objects to have temporal parts. My hand is a part of me; my five-year-old self is not.

The B-theory's radical departure from widely held commonsense beliefs about time can be taken as an objection to it. It is a theoretical virtue that, as far as possible, philosophical theories ought to avoid major conflict with widely held beliefs. However, this is not an absolute constraint. Commonsense beliefs are defeasible and can be defeated by scientific discoveries. We know, for example, that when a straight stick looks bent in water, it is not really bent. It merely appears that way as a result of the differential refraction of light through air and water. We know that the Earth is not flat and that the sun does not rotate around it. These scientific discoveries overthrew widely held commonsense beliefs to the contrary. In short, the fact that the B-theory conflicts with commonsense beliefs does not give us reason to reject it outright. There are other theoretical virtues that we must consider when evaluating metaphysical theories. The question of theory choice in metaphysics is not entirely unrelated to the question of theory choice in science. It is, at least in part, a matter of weighing up how well each theory does with respect to a number of theoretical virtues and constraints. Some of these considerations are: how well it fits with scientific and other empirical knowledge; how well it explains and predicts certain phenomena; and whether it is ad hoc or internally inconsistent. As we shall see, the B-theory does a better job in these respects than the A-theory.

The B-theory arguably has a response to at least one of these claims of conflict with ordinary commonsense beliefs: the claim that, according to the B-theory, time is static, not dynamic. There is a growing cohort of B-theorists who resist the charge that the B-theory is a static theory of time, and object to the conclusion that they are forced to admit that time does not pass.[31] According to these philosophers, temporal passage consists in there being a succession of times. The B-theoretic ontology of tenselessly existing times is more than adequate for accommodating passage, if that is what it amounts to. Savitt (2002) quotes Williams (1951) approvingly, who says that 'There is passage, but it is nothing extra. It is the mere happening of things, their strung-along-ness in the manifold'[32] (Williams, 1951: 463). Savitt concurs. 'True and literal passage is the ordered occurrence of (simultaneity sets of) events in the manifold' (Savitt, 2002: 157). Similarly, Norton: 'The passage of time is the presentation to our consciousness of the successive moments of the world' (Norton,

---

[31] See, for example, Savitt (2002), Dieks (2006), Dorato (2006b), Oaklander (2012), Deng (2013b), Leininger (2014) and Mozersky (2015).

[32] By 'manifold' Williams means the B-theoretic spread of events through space-time.

2010: 24). Mozersky agrees: 'The key point for the B-theorist is that there is nothing to temporal passage over and above ordinary change' (Mozersky, 2013: 181). I follow Deng (2017: 240) and call this account of temporal passage 'tenseless passage'.

Is tenseless passage an adequate account of temporal passage? As Savitt asks, 'Is this true and literal passage, however, truly and literally passage – the real whooshy, zingy thing that is so salient in our experience?' (Savitt, 2002: 157). Or is it, as John Earman remarks, a 'thin and yawn-inducing' sense of passage (Earman, 2008: 159)? As Pooley comments, 'If one wishes to label the successive occurrence of events "temporal passage" then, yes, time passes according to the B Theory' (Pooley, 2013: 326). We saw, in our discussion of A-theoretic attempts to accommodate what Skow (2015: 2) calls 'robust passage', the passage of the metaphysical privilege of presentness from one time to the next, that they had one of three outcomes, none of which is satisfactory. The first is essentially McTaggart's paradox: an attempt to combine A-determinations with temporal passage results in every moment possessing every incompatible A-determination. The second is that an account of robust passage ultimately requires a further temporal dimension (hyper-time), relative to which ordinary time can be said to pass. Lastly, attempting to avoid both contradiction and hyper-time, the A-theory finds itself unable to accommodate passage at all. The result is either a static, frozen distribution of A-determinations, with one moment metaphysically privileged as present, or a multitude of such distributions, with no mechanism for moving from one to another.

If the A-theory is unable to provide a satisfactory account of robust passage, perhaps tenseless passage, thin and yawn-inducing as it may be, is as good as it is going to get, metaphysically speaking. Certainly, there's no contradiction involved in tenseless passage. Few will deny that times are temporally related to each other and that events occur successively at those times. Lacking a privileged present, it fits with our best scientific theories about time. And yet, where is the 'whoosh and whiz'? (Falk, 2003: 211). Where is this 'something extra, something active and dynamic' (Williams, 1951: 460) that inspires all the metaphors expressing the flow of time? In other words, while tenseless passage may be coherent, the objection is that it fails to capture the felt experience of passage; it fails to properly account for that element of our temporal experience that leads us to posit temporal passage in the first place.

But here we reach something of an impasse. Tenseless passage is not enough for the A-theorist. It does not capture the truly dynamic nature of time. But no attempt to work this 'something extra' into a coherent metaphysical picture of time is successful, so it looks like we cannot have it. Let's approach the problem from a different angle, drawing on my reflections on metaphysical methodology and the two philosophical tendencies. We want our metaphysical enquiry to result in an account of the nature of time that is objectively true. But in recognition of the subject-relative tendency to understand time as it appears to us, such an account must also be able to explain human temporal experience and why it has the features that it does. This can be done by explaining how the combination of time as it is in itself, and creatures like us located within it, with our particular perceptual and cognitive faculties, can give rise to our temporal experience, and our beliefs and intuitions based upon it. I will defer discussion of B-theoretic accounts of temporal experience until Section 6. For now, I simply want to acknowledge the region in the space of possibilities that is constituted by combining tenseless passage with some account of our perceptual and cognitive apparatus, together with our temporal perspective, to explain how our temporal experience and the beliefs and intuitions that it gives rise to, arises.

5.2 Reasons in Favour of the B-Theory

The objection that the B-theory conflicts with ordinary commonsense beliefs about time constitutes a typical initial reaction. I suggested earlier that we ought to set that objection aside. In Section 5.3 I will consider some further philosophical objections to the B-theory. But I turn now to consider what can be said in its favour.

One immediate advantage of the B-theory is that it is not subject to any of the challenges and objections that plague the A-theory. McTaggart's argument showed that objective A-determinations conflict with temporal passage. The reality of the A-series requires exclusivity (only *this* moment is present!) and inclusivity (but *every* moment gets to be present!), but it cannot have them both (Price, 2011). The B-theory denies that there is a metaphysically privileged present moment and that this privilege passes from one moment to the next, so it has no need to reconcile these claims with each other. It thereby avoids the need to postulate a further temporal dimension, hyper-time, in order to accommodate robust temporal passage. Since it does not postulate robust temporal passage, it does not face the objection that there must be a rate at which time passes.

The final objection against the A-theory that I examined was that, if consistent, it is just as static as the B-theory. A consistent tensed description of the world is temporally oriented to one present moment, which gives us a static, frozen tensed reality. The B-theory has an advantage here, even if it does face the objection that it gives a static picture of time. The static A-theoretic picture is patently false; we are not stuck in a frozen present moment. The sense in which the B-theory is static must still be defended against the objection that it cannot accommodate ordinary change.[33] Subject to its ability to overcome that objection, the static B-theory, unlike the static A-theory, is not *obviously* false. According to the B-theory, presentness is a relational, indexical feature, such that every moment is present relative to itself. This is consistent with our occupying different times, having different temporal perspectives at those times, and referring to each of those times as present. From each temporal perspective we designate a different moment as present, and a different distribution of pastness, presentness and futurity, but since this is not a robust distribution of pastness, presentness and futurity, but merely a relational, indexical one, there is no contradiction involved.

The other major advantage of the B-theory is that it is consistent with science. It does not face the challenge of having to reject much of what we know about time from other sources. While the A-theory appears to be a better fit with ordinary temporal experience and commonsense beliefs about time, the B-theory is a better fit with science. Each theory thus has an advantage on one side of the divide between what common sense and science each tell us about time, but it also has some work to do to accommodate the other side of that divide. I believe that the task facing the B-theory in this regard is vastly more surmountable than that facing the A-theory. The B-theory can take as its starting point well confirmed and widely agreed upon scientific beliefs about time (Callender, 2017: 27). Given those beliefs, together with what we know about human cognition, psychology, and perceptual and rational faculties, we ought to be able to put together an explanation of why creatures like us would experience B-theoretic time the way we do.

Callender (2017) embarks on just such a project. To illustrate the rationale behind his strategy he describes Eddington's 'two tables' problem (Eddington, 1928). Eddington provocatively remarks that there is not just one table before him, but two: the manifest table of common sense and ordinary experience, and the scientific table, which has the features that science tells us that it has. The manifest table is the commonplace object we are familiar with. 'It has extension; it is comparatively permanent; it is coloured; above all it is *substantial*' (Eddington, 1928: xi). It is also textured, rigid and heavy. The scientific table lacks these features. It 'is mostly emptiness. Sparsely scattered in that emptiness are numerous electric charges rushing about with great speed; but their combined bulk amounts to less than a billionth of the bulk of the table itself' (Eddington, 1928: xii). These two representations of the table conflict, so on the face of it, cannot both be

---

[33] I consider that objection in Section 5.3.1.

true. But that's not what we would want to say here. We'd be more inclined to say that there's just one table, but we can model it, or represent it, in two different ways. 'For navigating through the macroscopic world of ordinary life, we represent it one way, and for doing physics, we represent it another way' (Callender, 2017: 25). We wouldn't reject one model as false. Instead, each represents the world as it is in itself, albeit in different ways and for different purposes.

How are the two models related? Can we explain how the familiar properties of the manifest table emerge out of the more unfamiliar properties of the scientific table? Callender suggests that we take the scientific table as our starting point and see if we can explain some of the manifest properties in terms of the scientific properties (Callender, 2017: 25). But physics alone won't be able to explain all of the manifest properties. To explain colour and texture we'll need to describe the human perceptual system and how the surface of the object interacts with it. How an object looks and feels to a subject depends in part on the nature of the perceptual faculties of the subject. Callender offers a similar proposal for explaining how we get from scientific to manifest time. If we embed a creature like us, an 'information gathering and utilising system' (Callender, 2017: 26) with our perceptual and cognitive faculties, into relativistic space-time, could we explain why that creature might model time as having the features of our folk theory of time? Our explanation would appeal to objective features of space-time. But it would also appeal to facts about the creature herself and how she interacts with her physical environment.

However complex and demanding such an explanation might be to arrive at, it is in principle an achievable goal. We have the resources of all the sciences, and we can put them to the task of explaining why creatures like us, embedded in a spatiotemporal world as described by science, would model time in the way we do. The task of the A-theorist, by contrast, looks insurmountable. Manifest time masks the nature of scientific time. It suggests that time has properties that, according to science, we know that it does not have. By taking manifest time as a starting point, the A-theorist is in the awkward position of having to reject much of what science has shown to be true. Rather than being able to appeal to scientific results and evidence, and work them in to a theory about the nature of time and temporal experience, she will find herself having to explain away scientific results and evidence or to reject them entirely.

The situation for the A-theorist is in fact worse than this suggests. Some A-theorists have attempted to reconcile their views with science (Smith, 1993; Tooley, 1997; Bourne, 2006). The most common way in which they do this is by accepting that, according to STR, there is no empirically detectable privileged present moment. But this is consistent with there being a *metaphysically* privileged present moment. This move makes the A-theory consistent with STR, but it does so at the cost of undermining what motivates it in the first place. As Miller (2013) puts it,

> [A-theories] are motivated by the thought that *prima facie*, and in the absence of contravening evidence, the way the world seems to us is a good guide to the way the world is. Sometimes the way the world seems to us to be is not the way that it is. Such discoveries, such as the empirical discoveries that underlie STR, present problems for [A-theories]. The issue they face is not that their views cannot be made consistent with STR, but rather, that the most natural-istically and scientifically respectable ways of doing so radically undermine the motivations for [them]. For in making the privileged present empirically undetectable, it becomes very difficult to see how the presence of such a present could be the explanation for our temporal phenomenology, the very thing that motivates [such] views to posit a privileged present in the first place. (Miller, 2013: 360)

In the choice between being a better fit with science, or with commonsense beliefs about time, the advantage lies with the former. As I noted earlier, each theory has a prima facie advantage in being better aligned than its opponent with either science or commonsense beliefs. But being better aligned with one means having to reconcile itself with the other. The A-theory's project of reconciliation looks, at the very least, deeply problematic. The B-theory's project of reconciliation, on the other hand, looks in principle achievable. If we get the scientific facts right, we will be in a position to explain why things appear to us in the way they do. And this will involve not just physics, but human psychology, cognition, perception, evolutionary biology and other fields, as well.

5.3 Objections to the B-Theory

5.3.1 If Time Is Static, How Does the B-Theory Account for Change?

The B-theory says that time is more like space than we ordinarily think. According to this objection, the B-theory takes this too far, so is unable to account for ordinary change; the change in properties that objects undergo. There are two ways of developing this objection. The first asks us to consider the four-dimensional block universe of the B-theory that is extended in three spatial dimensions and one temporal dimension. Considered as if from a perspective outside this block universe – an atemporal perspective – the entire history of the universe is laid out before us. Nothing about the universe considered in this way ever changes. It is a static array of objects and events spread out in space-time. As such, the objection goes, this model cannot accommodate ordinary change. Thinking of the objection in this way reflects the tension between being and becoming that has repeatedly emerged in philosophical discussions about the nature of time across the centuries. If all events are laid out in a temporal order, standing in fixed and unchanging relations to each other, how can this static picture accommodate the change and flux all around us? In my view, this objection either assumes that change must be A-theoretic in nature, and so begs the question, or it is a non sequitur. I'll take each option in turn.

The objection that nothing about the four-dimensional block universe ever changes assumes that change must be something that happens to the universe as a whole: that the universe undergoes 'coming to be' and 'passing away' or change in what exists. But change understood in this way can only be A-series change. It is not the change that ordinary objects undergo. That change can be accommodated by the four-dimensional block universe, as it consists in objects possessing different properties at different times. By taking change to be something more than that, the objection assumes that B-theoretic change is insufficient to constitute genuine change. It thus begs the question against the B-theory.

Another way of developing this response is to appeal to the different perspectives in play here. The objection asks us to consider the four-dimensional block universe as if from an atemporal perspective and then complains that nothing about the universe so considered ever changes. That may be right, but it doesn't follow that change does not take place *within* that universe. Within the universe, objects have different properties at different times and so they change. Nothing about this picture rules out the possibility that, if an observer were to adopt a temporal perspective within the universe and observe this change in properties of ordinary objects, it would appear to her as genuine change.

According to the second interpretation of this objection, the B-theoretic account of change is insufficiently different from spatial variation, and since spatial variation does not constitute change, neither does the temporal variation in properties that is B-theoretic change. An object changes, according to the B-theory, when it possesses a property at one time that it lacks at another.[34] The ripening tomato changes because it is green at one time and later it is red. But objects can also have different properties at different places. A tomato might be red on the side facing the sun but green on the side facing the wall. We saw in Section 3.1.1, in the discussion of McTaggart's objection to B-theoretic change, that the B-theory has a response to this objection. The B-theoretic account of change may be analogous to spatial variation, and indeed this is what we should

---

[34] There are different B-theoretic accounts of change, but the differences between them need not concern us here.

expect given that the temporal dimension is just one dimension of four-dimensional space-time. But the B-theorist can point to a relevant difference between the temporal dimension and any spatial dimension: it is the dimension along which causation operates. The objection is thus a non sequitur.

5.3.2 If All Times Are Equally Real, How Does the B-Theory Account for Free Will?

The B-theory says that all times are equally real. According to this objection, this claim is inconsistent with human free will. How can I be free to choose between options if my future choice exists? If it exists, does it not follow that it is already fixed, so I cannot do otherwise than act in that way? There are two options available to the B-theorist here. She could accept that there is a conflict between the reality of the future and the existence of free will, and deny that there is any free will. This would involve giving an account of why we *think* we have free will, that is, explaining the manifest features of our experience, which give rise to the widespread belief that we act freely. But this is arguably not an insurmountable problem, and furthermore it is faced not just by those who accept that the reality of the future precludes free will, but also by those who accept determinism, and believe that it precludes free will.

Alternatively, the B-theorist could reject the claim that the reality of the future conflicts with the existence of free will. On this response, a B-theoretic ontology does not entail that the future is fixed, in the sense that it cannot be affected by our present actions. The B-theory is committed to logical determinism: the doctrine that future tense statements have a determinate truth value. But this should not be confused with the much stronger doctrine, physical determinism, according to which, given the present total state of the universe and the laws of nature, only one future is possible. The B-theory is not committed to physical determinism. It is compatible with both physical determinism and indeterminism. The reality of future times does not determine whether what happens at those times is causally determined.

Logical determinism entails that there are truths about the future, but what those truths describe needn't be *causally* determined. Things could turn out the way they describe precisely because of our freely chosen actions. The future is causally dependent on the past, according to the B-theory, but many of those causes may well be free human actions. From the fact that there are truths about the future, it does not follow that future events are inevitable. According to Ryle (1954), this objection can be unpacked into a trivial but dull truth and an exciting but false proposition. The trivial but dull truth is that 'for anything that happens, if anyone had at any previous time made the guess that it would happen, his guess would have turned out correct' (Ryle, 1954: 22–23). The exciting but false proposition is 'that whatever happens is inevitable or doomed, and, what makes it sound even worse, logically inevitable or logically doomed' (Ryle, 1954: 23). From the claim that future times are real, it does not follow that what happens at those times is already fixed.

But what motivates the temptation to think that the reality of the future implies that we have no free will? I think one motivation lies with the notion of adopting an atemporal perspective on temporal reality, where all events are laid out in a fixed manifold. This encourages the thought that every time exists *now*, just as every frame of the film reel laid out before me exists now. It then seems natural to infer that, since future events exist now, what happens at them must be fixed now. But the atemporal perspective is a theoretical fiction; we cannot really adopt it. We can imagine ourselves adopting it, but we must be careful to ensure that this imaginative exercise includes the correct B-theoretic ontology: every time exists *tenselessly*, not simultaneously with every other time. When we consider the causes of a future event we should look to the events that happen just before it. There is no inconsistency in some of those earlier causes being free human actions. To think that the reality of a future event determines my present choice is to get the cause and effect the wrong way round. It is my present choice that causes the future event to turn out the way that it does.

5.3.3 If Time Is Not Tensed, Why Does Language Suggest That It Is?

Ordinary English enables its users to locate events in the past, present or future. In English, one linguistic means of doing this is grammatical tense, but there are others.[35] Grammatical tense is tied to the notion of a deictic centre; a reference point relative to which we can locate events in time, typically the moment of speech. It is generally accepted that all languages have some means of doing this (Sinha & Gärdenfors, 2014). Thus, languages in general recognise a distinction between past, present and future. Some A-theorists (Smith, 1993; Ludlow, 1999; Craig, 2000) have taken this to imply that there is, in reality, such a distinction that exists independently of any observer. The A-theory takes tensed language at face value (Prior, 1967). If a sentence appears to locate an event in the past, what it takes for that sentence to be true is for that event to be located in the past. For that to be the case, the past must be a genuine feature of

---

[35] See Crystal (2002) and Dyke (2013) for discussion of different linguistic means of locating events in the past, present or future.

temporal reality. The B-theory rejects the reality of tense, so it owes us an explanation of what makes tensed sentences true if not tensed facts, and why we think and speak as if tense is real if it isn't.

The standard B-theoretic explanation of what makes tensed sentences true is that they are made true by tenseless facts involving the temporal relation between an utterance and the event that it is about. An utterance of the sentence, 'The Spanish flu pandemic is past' is made true by the fact that the Spanish flu pandemic is earlier than the utterance of the sentence.[36] Tensed language plays an indexical role, locating events in terms of their temporal relations to the moment of utterance. It fixes the moment of utterance as the deictic centre, the 'present' moment, and locates other events with reference to it.

The B-theoretic explanation of why we think and speak as if tense is real is that much of our thought and talk is perspectival, or temporally self-locating, and this is necessary for us to navigate our way through the world and for successful timely action. If I have a class at 10:00am, my belief that I have a class at 10:00am will not cause me to head to the classroom unless I also believe that it is *now* nearly 10:00am. Tenseless beliefs, such as the belief that my class starts at 10:00am, are not sufficient to explain why we act *when* we do. Tensed beliefs are necessary for timely action. *True* tensed beliefs are necessary for *successful* timely action (Mellor, 1998: 58–66; Torre, 2010). Tensed beliefs are temporally self-locating because they locate events relative to one's own temporal location. In order to succeed in our actions, we need at least some beliefs that are not true at all times but only true when we have them. In order to get to my class on time I need the true tensed belief *My class starts in five minutes*, so that I can start walking towards the classroom and get there on time. And that belief is only true at 9:55am.

B-theorists argue that having true tensed beliefs has no implications for the existence of tense in reality. True tensed beliefs are made true by purely tenseless relational facts. The belief that *My class starts now* is made true by the tenseless relational fact that the start of my class is simultaneous with my having the belief. On this view, temporal reality is inherently tenseless, but in order to successfully navigate our way around it, we need true tensed (temporally self-locating), as well as tenseless, beliefs about it. The irreducibly tensed beliefs reflect the fact that we perceive the world always from a particular temporal perspective, but they have no implications for the existence of tense in reality.

---

[36] There are slight variations among B-theorists on the details of this account, but they need not concern us here.

Much more can be said about these, and other, objections to the B-theory, but I want to turn, in the next section, to what is perhaps the most compelling objection against it. This is that the B-theory conflicts with what our experience tells us time is like. Despite the problems facing the A-theory, the B-theory must be able to explain why, if time is not tensed, our temporal experience seems to tell us that it is.

6 Explaining Temporal Experience

We saw in Section 5.2 that while the A-theory appears to be a better fit with ordinary temporal experience and commonsense beliefs about time, the B-theory is a better fit with science. This leaves work to do for each theory. The A-theory must attempt to reconcile itself with science, while the B-theory must attempt to reconcile itself with ordinary experience and commonsense beliefs about time. My focus here is on the task facing the B-theory. Can it adequately account for features of our temporal experience, and the beliefs that they give rise to? Recall the goal of a metaphysical enquiry into the nature of time: to arrive at an account of the nature of time that is objectively true from a universal standpoint. That account must also accommodate the human-centred point of view, explaining the features of our temporal experience that do not appear in the objective account. Human temporal experience is, after all, a component of reality and so deserves an explanation as part of this project. In short, a metaphysical enquiry into the nature of time must accommodate both the subject-neutral tendency to understand the world as it is independently of us and the subject-relative tendency to understand the world as it appears to us.

I will focus on the two elements of our ordinary experience and commonsense beliefs that feature in our folk theory of time: the belief that there is an objective present moment, and the belief that time passes.[37] I take it that these beliefs are caused by features of our temporal phenomenology. It *seems* to us as though there is an objective present moment, and that time passes, so we *believe* that there is an objective present moment, and that time passes (Torrengo, 2017). These two elements of our temporal experience are often considered together, either as two aspects of a broader category of temporal experience per se, or one of them is taken to be a constituent of the other. Price (2011), for example, writes 'One major component of the intuitive idea of the passage of

---

[37] There are other elements of our ordinary temporal experience, and beliefs based on that experience, which I do not have the space to cover here. These include our asymmetric attitudes to past and future (Prior, 1959; Maclaurin & Dyke, 2002; Suhler & Callender, 2012; Callender, 2017), the so-called specious present (Dainton 2013), our experiences of duration and succession (Le Poidevin, 2007) and memory (Le Poidevin, 2007; Fernández, 2013).

time is that it involves a distinguished but continually variable "present moment'" (Price, 2011: 277). Similarly, Paul's reconstruction of the argument from temporal experience incorporates both elements, as she calls them, 'experiences as of nowness and as of the passage of events' (Paul, 2010: 333). In my view it is worth considering each of these elements separately, as they may have different explanations.

Torrengo (2018) agrees, arguing that, while obviously closely connected, these two features of experience are distinguishable (Torrengo, 2018: 1045), and it is important to distinguish them if we are interested in finding the most plausible explanations for them.[38] He criticises the view that there is some explanatory connection between presentness and passage; that the experience as of presentness can somehow explain the experience as of passage. He bases his criticism on an ambiguity in the literature between the perspectival and the dynamic understanding of tense. The term 'tense' has been used as a blanket term to cover both presentness (the perspectival interpretation) and passage (the dynamic interpretation). It is only when we unpick these two elements of tense that we can see that there is no explanatory connection between representing things as present and representing things as dynamic (Torrengo, 2018: 1046). It would be possible to have a perspectival representation without an associated dynamic representation, as we have in the case of space (Torrengo, 2018: 1053).

6.1 Experience as of a Privileged Present

It is a striking and powerful component of our temporal phenomenology that it seems to us as though the moment we occupy, the present moment, is somehow privileged and, what is more, it is shared. We all occupy the same present moment. In contrast, we each occupy our own 'here'. Subject to certain constraints it is up to us which spatial location we occupy, but we seem to have no choice about which temporal location we occupy. Which moment is present seems to be something that the world imposes on us, so it is natural to think that it is an objective, rather than merely perspectival, feature of the world. The fact that it seems to us as though we occupy a shared, mind-independent now is often appealed to in support of the A-theory. Things seem to us to be this way, so in the absence of reasons for thinking otherwise, we ought to take this component of our phenomenology to be veridical. Things *seem* to us this way, because they *are in fact* this way. We can represent this line of thought with the following argument, distilled from the more general argument from temporal experience in Section 4.2:

---

[38] See also Riggs (2017).

The Argument from Experience as of an Objective Present Moment
1. We have experiences as of an objectively privileged present moment.
2. If we have experiences as of an objectively privileged present moment, then any reasonable explanation for this relies on presentness being an objective feature of reality.
3. Therefore, presentness is an objective feature of reality.

The A-theorist, who endorses this argument, takes the phenomenal character of our experiences as of presentness to represent the way the world in fact is. The feeling as of an objective, privileged present is a representational feature of the content of our experience. I will label this view *representationalism* about objective presentness. Before considering B-theoretic responses to this argument, I want to suggest some reasons for being sceptical about the strength of the A-theorist's position.

A representationalist about objective presentness takes presentness to be part of the representational content of our experiences. But do we directly experience presentness? Is presentness a phenomenal property? There are reasons for doubting that it is. Mellor (1998: 16) points out that we sometimes have perceptual experiences of events that happened in the distant past, such as when we observe light from a distant star, yet there is no discernible difference between this and having a perceptual experience of an event that is (more or less) present. If it's not possible to distinguish perceptually between events even though they differ enormously in age, then the representational content of our experiences, it would seem, does not include a phenomenal property of being present

Relatedly, Le Poidevin (2007: 77–78) argues that there is a sense in which the claim that we perceive only the present is simply trivial. It is not clear that there is an interesting difference between perceiving something as present and just perceiving it. If, as Mellor argues, there is no discernible difference between perceptual experiences of past and present events, so that there is nothing standing in contrast with perceiving something as present, then it's hard to see what difference there is between simply perceiving and perceiving as present. It follows that there is no component of our experience that we can call 'presentness' that stands in need of explanation.

Following on from Le Poidevin's point, phenomenal properties generally serve to distinguish between different experiences. The phenomenal property *being soft* distinguishes my experience of touching a cushion from my experience of touching a table. But presentness does not play this role. Every experience I have is present, so presentness cannot discriminate one experience from another (Hestevold, 1990; Le Poidevin, 2007; Callender, 2008; Skow, 2011b). In particular, it cannot distinguish present from non-present experiences. Furthermore, if every experience

I have is present, how do I identify presentness? As Skow (2011b: 370–71) argues, suppose my Monday and Tuesday experiences are phenomenally identical, but only the Tuesday experiences are present. Do the Monday experiences feel different from the Tuesday experiences? Skow thinks not. Suppose on Monday I produce a complete and accurate description of the phenomenal character of my experiences, and I do the same on Tuesday. Skow remarks, 'I think it is obvious that the descriptions will be word-for-word the same' (Skow, 2011b: 371).

Finally, Prosser (2007, 2016) has argued, with respect to temporal passage, that it couldn't causally influence perceptual experiences, and so we couldn't experience it. I think a parallel case can be made for the property of presentness. Prosser's 'detector argument' asks whether there could be 'a physical device that could detect whether or not time was passing, and thus tell us whether or not the A-theory was true' (Prosser, 2016: 33). Perhaps a light would illuminate when the device detected temporal passage. But the A-series and the B-series contain the very same physical events in the very same order. It follows that, if the light on the detector illuminates at all, it will illuminate in both the A-series and the B-series. So no physical device could detect the passage of time. Furthermore, on any acceptable view of the relation between mind and body, 'if no physical system can detect the passage of time then neither can the human mind' (Prosser, 2016: 35). Consider a similar device designed to detect presentness. If the light on the detector illuminates at all, it will illuminate in both the A-series and the B-series. So no physical device could detect presentness. And if no physical system can detect presentness, then neither can the human mind.

So there are reasons to be sceptical about the A-theory's representationalism about our experiences as of objective presentness. How might a B-theorist respond to the argument from experience? It's an argument to the best explanation, so a natural response would be to reject the second premise, and offer alternative, B-theoretic explanations for these experiences. I will label approaches that fall into this category *illusionism* about objective presentness. They accept that we have these experiences, but argue that they are in some sense non-veridical or illusory. But the B-theorist could also reject the first premise. To do so would be to assert that the experiences we have are *not* experiences as of an objectively privileged present moment. I will label approaches that fall into this category *deflationism* about objective presentness. I take these two options in turn.

6.1.1 Illusionism about Objective Presentness

We seem to have no choice as to which moment we occupy, so it seems to us as though which moment is present is a feature that the world imposes upon us.

Perhaps it is this that leads us to think of it as an objective feature of the world. By contrast, where 'here' is, is more straightforwardly a relational, indexical feature that we ascribe to any location in which we happen to be situated. There are two issues to be explained here. First, why do we seem to have no choice about which moment we occupy, while we do have some choice over which spatial location we occupy? Second, why are we more inclined to take our temporal egocentric representations to be objective than our spatial egocentric representations?

Let's unpack the claim that we seem to have no choice about which moment we occupy, while we do have some choice over which spatial location we occupy. In the four-dimensional block universe of the B-theory, spatial and temporal locations cannot be considered in isolation from each other. We occupy *spatiotemporal* locations. Each of our world-lines follows a path through space-time, with each spatiotemporal location occupied having three spatial coordinates and one temporal coordinate. From a particular spatiotemporal location, I have some choice about which will be my next spatial coordinates, but I have no choice about which will be my next temporal coordinate. Callender (2017) refers to this as the 'mobility asymmetry' between time and space. 'The physical facts, taken together, imply that there is a sense in which we are . . . "stuck" in time in a way that we aren't "stuck" in space' (Callender, 2017: 222).

The mobility asymmetry is a contributing factor in the asymmetry between how we tend to treat temporally and spatially egocentric representations. The one-dimensionality of time ensures that we cannot observe other 'nows' in the way we can observe other 'heres'. It follows that it's much easier to accept that where 'here' is, is just one place among many and that other places will be 'here' for other observers. But why is there such widespread intersubjective agreement about when 'now' is? I remarked earlier that we all occupy the same present moment and this stands in need of explanation. But who is referred to by 'we' in this statement? According to the B-theory, all observers exist, no matter their temporal location, but 'we' cannot be referring to all observers whenever they are located. Instead, it picks out all observers who share a temporal location with a given utterance of this statement (Le Poidevin, 2007: 86). In a sense, the statement 'we all occupy the same present moment' is trivially true because 'we' refers to all those observers who occupy the same temporal location as the utterer of the statement.

But still this doesn't quite explain why we feel that egocentric temporal representations are objective, but we don't feel the same about egocentric spatial representations. After all, I can remark that all those located in Dunedin would assent to the statement 'Dunedin is here' and so we all share a common 'here'. But this would not tempt me to the conclusion that where here is, is an objective spatial feature. Callender (2017: 209) calls this the 'Representational Asymmetry'. Building on work by Butterfield (1984), Callender (2008, 2017) puts forward what I take to be the best explanation of this asymmetry.[39] Observation, belief-formation and communication, at the macroscopic level, all take place over very short, finite temporal durations. There is a time lag, albeit a very small one, between our observations and our forming beliefs about those observations, and there is a further small time lag between our forming beliefs and our communicating those beliefs to others. The time lag between observation and belief-formation is typically too small for anything to happen to render those beliefs false. This implies that we can reliably form beliefs and communicate about macroscopic objects without including time stamps (e.g. dates or clock times) (Callender, 2017: 215). As a result, we can treat *now* as a monadic property of an event, rather than a relational one between that event and a B-time. But in our use of spatial indexicals like 'here', we are aware that the place I designate as *here* is different from the place you designate as *here*, so we are not inclined to treat *here* as a monadic property of a place.

Following Callender and Butterfield, we can see that there are B-theoretic resources sufficient to explain our experience as of objective presentness, so the second premise of the argument from experience can be challenged.

6.1.2 Deflationism about Objective Presentness

Deflationism about objective presentness rejects the first premise of the argument from temporal experience, that we have experiences as of an objectively privileged present moment. How are we to understand this 'privilege'? Is it any more than the indexical, egocentric sense in which the moment that I am experiencing is the moment at which I am doing the experiencing? The moment is both the object of my experience and the subjective perspective from which I experience it. A-theorists insist that it is something more than this, but on what grounds? Do we directly experience, or detect, the privilege? Arguably not.[40] For any given moment, we simply experience what occurs at that moment, and

---

[39] There are other alternative explanations of our experience as of objective presentness that would fit into this category. Kriegel (2015) offers an account of our perception of objects and events as present that makes presentness not a part of the content of what is perceived but a mode of perception. The presentness, on this view, is attitudinal rather than representational. Similarly, Brogaard and Gatzia (2015) argue that we perceive the world as tensed, but this property is weakly emergent from static temporal properties, in much the same way as our perceptions of properties such as colour and texture can be veridical even though those properties are not instantiated at the fundamental level.

[40] And as we saw earlier, an argument can be made that we *couldn't* experience or detect it.

at that moment, we take it to be privileged. But the same goes for every other moment that we experience. Any reason for thinking that this moment is privileged over every other moment applies equally to every other moment. Recall the tension between exclusivity (*this* moment is privileged!) and inclusivity (*every* moment gets to be privileged!).

The deflationist can argue that it's possible for our experiences to be the way they are, but for those experiences *not* to be experiences as of an objectively privileged present moment. Instead, our experiences are of events at a particular moment from the perspective of that very moment. Unlike the illusionist, the deflationist does not take our experiences to be illusory or misleading. We are embedded in time, so we encounter the world, and represent it, always from the perspective of a particular time. Its perspectival nature affects the experience and gives it a certain character. The deflationist can argue that the character given to our experiences by the fact that they are had from a particular temporal perspective is that the temporal perspective occupied is taken to be privileged. But that privilege amounts to nothing more than the egocentric perspective so occupied.

Consider a spatial analogy. There is a difference in the character of perceptual experience when looking at a representation of a city in a smartphone mapping 'app', using 'map view' and 'street view'. The map view shows the location of all the streets and landmarks and how they are related to each other. The street view shows how a location looks from that particular location with that particular orientation. The two views have a different character, but they are views of the same spatial region; they represent the same facts. What contributes to the character of the street view is the position and orientation of the viewer. But the position and orientation of the viewer is not an extra fact over and above the fact that it is the spatial location occupied by the viewer. There is objective content, represented by the map view, which remains invariant regardless of one's particular location. And then there are embedded perspectives within that objective content. Each street view image gives a different representation of the same objective content. As Ismael (2011) notes, 'Part of knowing how to interpret the visual field – that is, how to distill out its objective content, how to separate what it is telling you about the world from what it is telling you about your position in it – is knowing to anticipate and account for changes in appearance due to perspective' (Ismael, 2011: 479).

The deflationist takes a similar view of our temporal experiences as of an objectively privileged present moment. Our experiences are imbued with a character that comes from the fact that they are had from a particular temporal perspective. That character can be explained without recourse to any metaphysical or ontological privilege. It is simply what it is like to encounter the world from an embedded temporal perspective. The deflationist can argue that the experience of a moment as present is nothing more than the experience of reality from an embedded temporal perspective.

Both illusionism and deflationism about our experiences as of an objectively privileged present are plausible and workable positions. But explanation of this element of our temporal experience only gets us so far. Recall the static, frozen A-series, which is a false representation of temporal reality. We may be able to adequately explain our experience as of a privileged present, but we must also explain our experience as of a dynamic, continual changing of temporal perspectives. Can the B-theory explain this element of our experience?

6.2 Experience as of Temporal Passage

That we do have something like an experience as of passage has been widely accepted by both B-theorists and A-theorists.[41] Recent empirical work supports this assumption (Latham et al., 2021; Shardlow et al., 2021).[42] Nevertheless, a growing number of B-theorists now reject it.[43] Just like our experience as of a privileged present moment, this is a striking and powerful component of our temporal phenomenology. It too is commonly appealed to in support of the A-theory. Things seem to us to be this way, so in the absence of reasons for thinking otherwise, we ought to take this component of our phenomenology to be veridical. Things *seem* to us this way, because they *are in fact* this way. We can represent this line of thought with the following argument:

The Argument from Experience as of Temporal Passage
1. We have experiences as of temporal passage.
2. If we have experiences as of temporal passage, then any reasonable explanation for this relies on temporal passage being an objective feature of reality.
3. Therefore, temporal passage is an objective feature of reality.

The A-theorist, who endorses this argument, takes the phenomenal character of our experiences as of temporal passage to represent the way the world in fact is. The feeling as of temporal passage is a representational feature of the content of our experience. I will label this view *representationalism* about temporal passage. Just as we saw with representationalism about objective presentness,

---

[41] See, for example, Gale (1968), Lucas (1973), Schlesinger (1982), Craig (2000), Prosser (2007), Le Poidevin (2007) and Paul (2010).

[42] Latham et al. (2021) do not argue specifically for this conclusion but their data support it.

[43] See, for example, Bardon (2013), Deng (2013b), Leininger (2014), Frischhut (2015), Farr (2020b). This view will be examined in Section 6.2.2.

there are reasons for being sceptical about the strength of representationalism about temporal passage.

Prosser's 'detector argument', outlined earlier, undermines the view that temporal passage is a representational feature of the content of our experience. It is designed to show that experience fails to favour the A-theory over the B-theory; that experience would be just as it actually is whether the A-theory or the B-theory were true (Prosser, 2016: 42). But his 'multi-detector argument' is designed to show that the passage of time cannot be experienced at all (Prosser, 2016: 42–54). He argues that, unlike ordinary phenomenal qualities such as being red, or being soft, temporal passage is not capable of standing in the right kind of relation to a detecting system so that it could be detected. Minimally, in order for a detector to indicate the presence of some feature, f, of the physical world, it must be causally related to the presence of f, and detection of f must be counterfactually dependent on the presence of f. Prosser argues that, whereas these conditions can be met by ordinary physical phenomena, temporal passage cannot stand in the requisite causal or counterfactual relations to any detecting system. Now, Prosser's argument has been challenged (e.g. Skow, 2011b), but at the very least it establishes that temporal passage is relevantly different from ordinary phenomenal qualities, to the extent that we ought not to accept without question the claim that our experience as of passage is, or even could be, veridical.

Another reason for being sceptical of the representationalist's position is that, just like the experience as of presentness, the experience as of passage does not serve to distinguish some experiences from others (Prosser, 2013). If any experience has the phenomenal quality of passage, they all do. So passage does not function like ordinary phenomenal qualities, which gives us grounds for doubting that it could be veridical. What would experience be like in the absence of passage? If passage is part of the representational content of experience, we should be able to give a satisfactory answer to this question, but it's not clear that we could do so.

So there are reasons to be sceptical of the A-theorist's representationalist account of our experiences as of passage. I turn now to examine how a B-theorist might respond to this argument. I will label those who reject the first premise *deflationists* about passage, and those who reject the second premise *illusionists* about passage.

6.2.1 Illusionism about Temporal Passage

Illusionism about temporal passage accepts that we have experiences as of passage, but holds that that experience is non-veridical; there are better explanations for it than that temporal passage is an objective feature of temporal reality. An early example of this view is Mellor's (1998: 122–23) account in terms of the way our memories accumulate. Our perceptions are accompanied by memories of earlier perceptions, and some of those memories are of earlier perceptions that are also accompanied by memories. Suppose you are in a boring lecture, and you are watching the progress of the minute hand around the clock. You see the clock say 10:15am. You look back a few minutes later and see it says 10:19am, but that perception is accompanied by the memory of seeing the clock say 10:15am. When you next look, you see it says 10:23am and that perception is accompanied by the memory of seeing it say 10:19am while also remembering it say 10:15am.

This account of the way our memories accumulate may well contribute to an explanation of some elements of our temporal experience, such as the experience of our life unfolding towards the future, but it is inadequate as an account of our experience as of temporal passage. There is a sense in which our experience as of temporal passage is direct and not merely inferred on the basis of memories. We directly see the sands fall through the hourglass and hear the notes of a melody, and this experience is itself imbued with transience. It does not rely on memories of other perceptions for its transient character.[44]

A now well-known and much discussed proposed explanation of the experience as of passage is offered by Paul (2010). Her account is intended to explain how our experience as of passage could arise as a result of the way our brains process and interpret sequences of static inputs. She appeals to the phenomenon of apparent motion. It is well-confirmed that the brain performs some sort of interpretative function when presented with sequences of static inputs, generating the impression of motion. Flipbook animation gives the impression of a figure in motion from the observation of a sequence of static images of that figure. Time-lapse photography, made up of sequences of static images run in quick succession, likewise gives the impression of motion or change. The brain takes these sequences of static images as input and processes them into an impression of smooth and continuous change. It gives us the illusion of the animated character of qualitative change.

Paul focuses her explanation of the experience as of passage on the results of an experiment known as 'colour phi'. Subjects are presented with a screen on which a dot appears on the left, then quickly disappears, followed by a dot appearing on the right, which quickly disappears. This process repeats in quick succession. The dot on the left-hand side is a different colour, say red, from the dot on the right-hand side, say green. When presented with these stimuli,

---

[44] See Prosser (2016) and Brogaard and Gatzia (2015) for further criticism of Mellor's explanation.

subjects report seeing a single dot moving from left to right and back again across the screen. Since the stimuli only appear at the left and right, researchers hypothesise that the brain supplies the missing elements to give the impression of continuous motion of a single, persisting dot. Subjects also report that the dot changes colour at about the half-way point in its 'motion' across the screen. Since there are no stimuli other than those at the left and right, the hypothesis is that the brain is responsible for supplying these missing elements about the change in colour of the dot.

Paul argues that essentially the same thing happens with our perception of the static inputs of the B-theorist's world, giving rise to our experience as of passage. When we observe ordinary change, our brains are presented with sequences of contrasting static inputs; impressions of an object possessing first one property and then another. The brain processes this series of inputs and produces a mental representation of a persisting object changing in an animated or flowing way. According to Paul, there is no flow or passage in the world. The brain creates the illusion of flow by processing sequences of inputs from earlier and later temporal stages (Paul, 2010: 352).

Paul's view has been criticised. Callender, for example, argues that her appeal to colour phi can at best demonstrate that we can't infer from motion qualia that something actually moves (2017: 239). He denies that the B-theorist's block universe is relevantly similar to colour phi, because it contains change. There is genuine change, such as when a leaf falls from a tree, and there is apparent change, such as the colour phi dots. When we add experiencing subjects to the world, there is a range of alternatives. Sometimes we genuinely perceive motion, so our motion qualia are veridical. But errors can occur. We sometimes have motion qualia in the absence of real motion, such as in colour phi, and we sometimes have real motion but no motion qualia, such as when the motion is too slow for us to detect. Callender argues that attempting to explain all our experiences as of passage in terms of colour phi obscures these differences (Callender, 2017: 240).

I think Callender is right to argue that colour phi cannot supply all the materials for explaining our experience as of passage and also that Paul's account obscures the difference between real and apparent change. Paul is effectively arguing by analogy from colour phi to our entire temporal phenomenology. Callender denies that the B-theoretic world is relevantly similar to colour phi because it contains change. However, in Paul's defence, B-theoretic change is, arguably, relevantly similar to colour phi because it consists in spatiotemporal variation in properties. Suppose a tomato, O, is green at t_1 and red at t_2. According to the B-theory, O changes from green to red. We call this change because it is one and the same object that undergoes the change in properties, and that is what is lacking in colour phi, where there is no persisting entity that is first red on the left and then green on the right. However, on one B-theoretic account of change, what makes it the case that O changes from green to red is that it has a t_1 temporal part that is green and a t_2 temporal part that is red. In that case, strictly speaking, there is no persisting entity, O, that is first green and then red, so the ripening tomato *is* relevantly similar to colour phi.[45]

Nevertheless, I think there is a weakness in the overall strategy of the illusionist, which is that by conceding that our experience as of passage is illusory, it concedes too much. Paul is quite explicit that she takes our experience to be illusory: 'Thus, according to the [illusionist], there is no real flow or animation in changes that occur across time. Rather, a stage of one's brain creates the *illusion* of such flow' (Paul, 2010: 352). But if our experience as of passage is illusory, it is not like other illusions. For one thing, it is ubiquitous. It characterises all of our experience, to the extent that we couldn't say what it would be like to not be experiencing the passage illusion. Illusions are not typically ubiquitous. We can normally control and eradicate them, so we can distinguish between when we are subject to them and when we are not (Norton, 2010). Consider the illusion of seeing a straight stick in water that appears bent. We can remove the stick from the water so that it no longer appears bent. Furthermore, we can usually identify the mechanism that brings about an illusion, allowing us to control for its effect. If the experience as of passage is illusory, however, then *all* of our experience is illusory. It seems implausible that all of our experience should be subject to such widespread and systematic error. The claim that our experience as of passage is illusory creates two problems. First, it is implausible to hold that such a fundamental feature of our temporal experience is illusory. Second, even if we accept that it is illusory, it does not behave like other illusions to which we are subject, so it would seem not to be subject to the same kind of explanation.

But there is, I think, *something* right about Paul's view, which is that she appeals to results from cognitive science and psychology about how the brain operates in developing her explanation of our experience as of passage. It is an attempt to combine an objective account of temporal reality (the B-theory) with an explanation of how creatures like us would experience that temporal reality from a perspective embedded within it. Perhaps we can incorporate this element of the illusionist approach, while jettisoning the claim that this experience is illusory. One way of doing that would be to take issue with the first premise of

---

[45] For further criticisms of Paul's view see Deng (2013c), Hoerl (2014), Prosser (2016) and Torrengo (2017).

the argument, and deny that we have experiences as of temporal passage at all. It's worth noting that all of Paul's examples of our experience as of passage are examples of our experience of motion and change. Perhaps the B-theorist can argue that we have experiences of motion, change and succession, all of which can be explained using B-theoretic resources, but there is nothing more to our alleged experiences as of passage than these experiences of motion, change and succession. The B-theorist can thus appeal to the resources of cognitive science, neuroscience and psychology to explain the character of our experience, but without endorsing the claim that our experience is all illusory.

6.2.2 Deflationism about Temporal Passage

Is it plausible to reject the premise that we have experiences as of temporal passage? One way to do so, as I began to suggest earlier, would be to claim that our alleged experiences as of passage are nothing more than our experiences of ordinary change and motion. Consider how the experience as of passage is commonly described:

> We just *see* time passing in front of us, in the movement of a second hand around a clock, or the falling of sand through an hourglass, or indeed any motion or change at all. (Le Poidevin, 2007: 76)

> I step out of my house into the morning air and feel the cool breeze on my face. I feel the freshness of the cool breeze now, and, as the breeze dies down, I notice that time is passing. (Paul, 2010: 1)

What more is there to these descriptions than a perception of ordinary change or motion? We *see* the second hand move around the clock; we *feel* the cool breeze. The representationalist insists that there is more to the experience as of temporal passage than just an experience of ordinary qualitative change, but what precisely is this additional element? Descriptions of this alleged experience typically fall into one of two categories. They are either highly metaphorical, or they describe nothing more than the phenomenal quality associated with perceiving ordinary qualitative change or motion, such as the aforementioned descriptions given by Le Poidevin and Paul. Neither type of description conveys any metaphysically robust claims about the nature of passage. Consider, for example, Williams's (1951: 466) attempt to capture the representationalist's reasoning from experience to the reality of passage:

> It is simply that we *find* passage, that we are immediately and poignantly involved in the jerk and whoosh of process, the felt flow of one moment into the next ... Here is the shore whence the youngster watches the golden mornings swing toward him like serried bright breakers from the ocean of

the future. Here is the flood on which the oldster wakes in the night to shudder at its swollen black torrent cascading him into the abyss. (Williams, 1951: 460)

Such 'enthusiastic metaphors of passage' (Williams, 1951: 466) are just that – harmless metaphors that add no more of any substance to an account of our experience than is captured by tenseless passage. The literal truth underlying these metaphors is adequately captured by the resources of the B-theory. Similarly, descriptions of experiences as of passage that describe nothing over and above experiences of ordinary motion and change can also be accounted for using just B-theoretic resources.

The deflationist position has been gaining traction and adherents in recent years. Frischhut (2015) rejects the claim that there is an experience as of temporal passage in need of explanation at all. We do not, she insists, experience passage in experiencing change (Frischhut, 2015: 146).[46] Deng (2013b) and Leininger (2014) both argue that there is a B-theoretic notion of passage based on succession. Unlike Frischhut, they accept that we *do* experience passage, but argue that it is nothing more than the experience of ordinary change or succession. Fundamentally, I think these are two different ways of expressing the same view. What Frischhut denies is that we experience robust passage. Deng and Leininger deny this too. Deng and Leininger argue that we experience succession and change, and they call this the experience as of passage. Frischhut agrees that we experience succession and change, but chooses not to call it an experience as of passage.

Recall the notion of tenseless passage, discussed in Section 5.1, which is simply the B-theoretic succession of events and moments. We saw there that tenseless passage may very well be as good as it gets if we want to incorporate any kind of temporal passage into our metaphysical theory of time. Deng and Leininger both argue that our experience of successions of events, or of objects undergoing ordinary change, is all that our experiences as of passage amount to. As we saw in Section 4, attempts to accommodate robust passage into a metaphysical theory of time are plagued with problems. If these attempts are ultimately unsuccessful, then metaphysically robust passage cannot be responsible for our experiences as of passage. In that case, tenseless passage is a better candidate to account for our experiences as of passage than metaphysically robust passage. As Deng argues, 'uncontroversial elements of the B-theory straightforwardly ground a veridical sense of passage' (Deng, 2013b: 713).

Hoerl (2014) argues similarly that there is no such phenomenology of robust passage in the first place. But there is a specific structural aspect of the

---

[46] See also Farr (2020b).

phenomenology of perceptual experiences of movement and change that can explain how we might mistakenly think there is (Hoerl, 2014: 188). He appeals to the difference between indirectly perceiving change, as happens, for example, when we observe the hands on a clock displaying 2:15pm while recalling them displaying 2:00pm, and directly perceiving change, as happens when we observe the second hand of a clock moving around the clock face (see also Riggs, 2017). The mistake we make, he argues, is to conflate the more animated experience involved in directly perceiving change with something over and above simple, ordinary change.

An obvious advantage of this view is that we can accept that our temporal experience is veridical without admitting the existence of anything metaphysically problematic, like robust passage. Furthermore, the position of the representationalist A-theorist begins to look increasingly like simple 'table thumping'. In the face of the deflationist's view that the B-theory has the resources to accommodate everything about our experience, the representationalist insists that there is more to our experience than the B-theory can provide. But what more is there? The representationalist cannot say.

Conversely, it is open to an opponent of deflationism to argue that, at least in some of its guises, it is too revisionary. It involves denying what most people believe is a basic fact about our experience. Hoerl's view, for example, is that we are simply mistaken when we conflate our direct perceptions of motion and change with something metaphysically more robust. I do not believe this criticism is fatal to deflationism, as the claim that we are mistaken about the nature of our experiences is not essential to it. The views of Deng, Leininger and Frischhut, for example, do not involve that claim. They claim instead that our experiences of change and motion *just are* experiences as of passage.

But the criticism is not fatal to deflationism even if it is committed to saying that we are mistaken about this element of our experience. Scientific discoveries have taught us that we are 'mistaken' about many elements of our experience. Recall Eddington's 'two tables', discussed in Section 5.2. Our experience tells us that the table is rigid, textured, coloured and heavy, but these properties are not instantiated by the table when we give a scientific description of it. The scientific description tells us that the table is mostly made up of empty space and charged particles moving at great speed. Our response to this situation is not to say that our ordinary experience is mistaken, but rather to say that we can model, or represent, the table in two different ways. The deflationist can make a similar move here. We can model temporal reality in two different ways. The metaphysical model is B-theoretic, incorporating no privileged present and no temporal passage. The model generated by ordinary experience represents it as dynamic and as having a privileged present. It remains for the B-theorist to explain precisely how creatures like us, with our peculiar physical, psychological and cognitive makeup, when embedded in a B-theoretic temporal reality, would model that reality in the way that we do. However, progress is already well underway in that regard.[47]

6.3 Conclusion

The B-theorist owes us an explanation of our experiences as of objective presentness and passage, given that she denies that temporal reality includes either objective presentness or passage. The illusionist accepts that we have these experiences, but denies that positing objective presentness and passage provides the best explanation for them, offering alternative explanations. The deflationist denies that we have these experiences and offers alternative explanations for why we think we do. There is a sense in which the illusionist and the deflationist are not in conflict with each other. They are both attempting to deliver an explanation of the elements of our experience that lead to our folk theory of time. Both can appeal to the metaphysical resources of the B-theory as well as to the findings of cognitive science, neuroscience, psychology and other sciences, to explain why creatures like us experience B-theoretic temporal reality in the way that we do.

Recall the goal of a metaphysical enquiry into the nature of time: to provide an account of the nature of time that is objectively true. Such an account must accommodate what science and metaphysics tell us about the nature of time, but it must also be able to explain features of our temporal experience. If the B-theory is right, then prima facie time lacks some features that our experience tells us that it possesses. But this apparent conflict can be resolved by explaining how the very same temporal reality can be modelled objectively, by science and metaphysics, or subjectively, from an embedded temporal perspective. These two different models can be fully explained using only the resources of the B-theory together with those of the special sciences. The B-theory thus attempts to do justice to both philosophical tendencies: to understand time as it is in itself, and to understand it as it appears to us.

From the fact that the B-theoretic account of time does not include objective presentness or temporal passage, we should not infer that our temporal experience is somehow illusory or mistaken. Rather, our temporal experience is just what we should expect if creatures like us, with our peculiar physical and psychological makeup, are embedded within that B-theoretic temporal reality, and encounter it, and interact with it, always from particular temporal perspectives.

---

[47] See, for example, Callender, (2017), Power (2018), Arstila et al. (2019) and Hoerl & McCormack (2019).

7 Concluding Remarks

We began by looking at the apparently unavoidable tensions that arise when thinking about time. My goal has been to diagnose these tensions as stemming from two philosophical tendencies: the subject-neutral tendency to provide an account of time from an objective, or universal standpoint, and the subject-relative tendency to provide an account of time as we encounter it. Prima facie, these two tendencies generate accounts that are in conflict. Time, from our anthropocentric point of view, has a privileged present moment and a dynamic quality. Attempting to incorporate these features into the objective account of time, as the A-theory tries to do, leads to insurmountable problems. The more promising objective account, the B-theory, faces the challenge of explaining why, if time lacks these features, we seem to experience it as if it has them.

The challenge to the B-theory of explaining these features of our temporal experience is one that has been taken up by philosophers in greater numbers in recent years. Those involved have increasingly appealed to work being carried out on our temporal experience and temporal phenomenology in disciplines such as psychology, neuroscience and cognitive science. And this, I believe, is as it should be. No metaphysical account of the nature of time can be complete unless it explains why we experience time the way we do, as well as how it is, independently of us. How we experience time is, after all, a feature of reality, no less than the nature of time as it is independently of us. And work in the special sciences has made great progress in investigating and explaining our temporal experience and phenomenology. The most fruitful way to proceed is to incorporate both philosophical tendencies in developing a scientifically informed metaphysical account of the nature of time.

References

Arstila, V., Bardon, A., Power, S. E. & Vatakis, A. eds. (2019). *The Illusions of Time: Philosophical and Psychological Essays on Timing and Time Perception*. Cham, Switzerland: Palgrave Macmillan.

Augustine. (1953). *Confessions*. Washington, DC: Catholic University of America Press.

Bardon, A. (2013). *A Brief History of the Philosophy of Time*. Oxford: Oxford University Press.

Bigelow, J. (1996). Presentism and properties. In J. E. Tomberlin ed., *Philosophical Perspectives, 10, Metaphysics*, Oxford: Blackwell Publishers, pp. 35–52.

Boccardi, E. (2015). If it ain't moving it shall not be moved. *Topoi*, **34**, 171–85.

Bourne, C. (2006). *A Future for Presentism*. Oxford: Oxford University Press.

Broad, C. D. (1923). *Scientific Thought*, London: Kegan Paul, Trench, Trubner.

Broad, C. D. (1938). *An Examination of McTaggart's Philosophy*, vol. II. Cambridge: Cambridge University Press.

Brogaard, B. & Gatzia, D. E. (2015). Time and time perception. *Topoi*, **34**, 257–63.

Butterfield, J. (1984). Seeing the present. *Mind*, **93**(370), 161–76.

Callender, C. (2000). Shedding light on time. *Philosophy of Science*, **67**, S587–99.

Callender, C. (2008). The common now. *Philosophical Issues*, **18**(1), 339–61.

Callender, C. (2011). Time's ontic voltage. In A. Bardon, ed., *The Future of the Philosophy of Time*. Routledge, pp. 73–94.

Callender, C. (2017). *What Makes Time Special?* Oxford: Oxford University Press.

Cameron, R. P. (2015). *The Moving Spotlight: An Essay on Time and Topology*. Oxford: Oxford University Press.

Castañeda, H.-N. (1967). Indicators and quasi-indicators. *American Philosophical Quarterly*, **4**, 85–100.

Christensen, F. (1974). McTaggart's paradox and the nature of time. *Philosophical Quarterly*, **24**, 289–99.

Conee, E. & Sider, T. (2014). *Riddles of Existence: A Guided Tour of Metaphysics: New Edition*. Oxford: Clarendon Press.

Correia, F. & Rosenkranz, S. (2018). *Nothing to Come: A Defence of the Growing Block Theory of Time*. Synthese Library: Springer.

Craig, W. L. (1998). McTaggart's paradox and the problem of temporary intrinsics. *Analysis*, **58**, 122–27.

Craig, W. L. (2000). *The Tensed Theory of Time: A Critical Examination*. Dordrecht: Kluwer Academic Publishers.

Crisp, T. (2003). Presentism. In M. J. Loux & D. W. Zimmerman, eds., *The Oxford Handbook of Metaphysics*. Oxford: Oxford University Press, pp. 211–45.

Crisp, T. (2004). On presentism and triviality. In D. Zimmerman, ed., *Oxford Studies in Metaphysics*, vol. 1. Oxford: Oxford University Press, pp. 15–20.

Crisp, T. (2005). Review of *The Ontology of Time*, by L. Nathan Oaklander (New York: Prometheus Books, 2004). *Notre Dame Philosophical Reviews*, https://ndpr.nd.edu/reviews/the-ontology-of-time/

Crisp, T. (2007). Presentism and the grounding objection. *Noûs*, **41**(1), 90–109.

Crystal, D. (2002). Talking about time. In K. Ridderbos, ed., *Time*. Cambridge: Cambridge University Press, pp. 105–25.

Dainton, B. (2013). The perception of time. In H. Dyke & A. Bardon, eds., *A Companion to the Philosophy of Time*. Malden, MA: Wiley-Blackwell, pp. 389–409.

Dieks, D. (2006). Becoming, relativity and locality. In D. Dieks, ed., *The Ontology of Spacetime*. Amsterdam: Elsevier, pp. 157–76.

Deng, N. (2013a). Fine's McTaggart, temporal passage, and the A versus B-debate. *Ratio*, **26**, 19–34.

Deng, N. (2013b). Our experience of passage on the B-theory. *Erkenntnis*, **78**, 713–26.

Deng, N. (2013c). On explaining why time seems to pass. *The Southern Journal of Philosophy*, **51**(3), 367–82.

Deng, N. (2017). Temporal experience and the A versus B debate. In I. Phillips, ed., *The Routledge Handbook of Philosophy of Temporal Experience*. New York: Routledge, pp. 239–48.

Dorato, M. (2006a). The irrelevance of the presentist/eternalist debate for the ontology of Minkowski spacetime. In D. Dieks, ed., *The Ontology of Spacetime*. Oxford: Elsevier, pp. 93–109.

Dorato, M. (2006b). Absolute becoming, relational becoming and the arrow of time: Some non-conventional remarks on the relationship between physics and metaphysics. *Studies in History and Philosophy of Modern Physics*, **37**, 559–76.

Dummett, M. (1960). A defence of McTaggart's proof of the unreality of time. *Philosophical Review*, **69**, 497–504.

Dyke, H. (2001). The pervasive paradox of tense. *Grazer Philosophische Studien*, **62**, 103–24.

Dyke, H. (2002). McTaggart and the truth about time. In C. Callender, ed., *Time, Reality and Experience*. Royal Institute of Philosophy Supplement, **50**. Cambridge: Cambridge University Press, pp. 137–52.

Dyke, H. (2008). *Metaphysics and the Representational Fallacy*. London: Routledge.

Dyke, H. (2011). On methodology in the metaphysics of time. In A. Bardon, ed., *The Future of the Philosophy of Time*. New York: Routledge, pp. 169–87.

Dyke, H. (2013). Time and tense. In H. Dyke & A. Bardon, eds., *A Companion to the Philosophy of Time*. Malden, MA: Wiley-Blackwell, pp. 328–44.

Dyke, H. (2021a). Weak neo-Whorfianism and the philosophy of time. *Mind & Language*, https://doi.org/10.1111/mila.12339

Dyke, H. (2021b). Review of K. A. Taylor, *Meaning Diminished: Toward Metaphysically Modest Semantics*. Oxford: Oxford University Press, 2019. *Philosophical Review*, **130**(3), 459–63.

Earman, J. (2008). Reassessing the prospects for a growing block model of the universe. *International Studies in the Philosophy of Science*, **22**, 135–64.

Eddington, A. S. (1928). *The Nature of the Physical World*. Cambridge: Cambridge University Press.

Falk, A. (2003). Time plus the whoosh and whiz. In A. Jokić & Q. Smith eds., *Time, Tense and Reference*. Cambridge, MA: MIT Press, pp. 211–50.

Falvey, K. (2010). The view from nowhen: The McTaggart-Dummett argument for the unreality of time. *Philosophia*, **38**, 297–312.

Farr, M. (2020a). C-theories of time: On the adirectionality of time. *Philosophy Compass*, **12**, 1–17.

Farr, M. (2020b). Explaining temporal qualia. *European Journal for Philosophy of Science*, **10**(8), 1–24. https://doi.org/10.1007/s13194-019-0264-6

Fernández, J. (2013). Memory. In H. Dyke & A. Bardon, eds., *A Companion to the Philosophy of Time*. Malden, MA: Wiley-Blackwell, pp. 432–43.

Fine, K. (2005). Tense and reality. In K. Fine, ed., *Modality and Tense: Philosophical Papers*. Oxford: Oxford University Press, pp. 261–320.

Fine, K. (2006). The reality of tense. *Synthese*, **150**(3), 399–414.

Forbes, G. A. (2015). Accounting for experiences as of passage: Why topology isn't enough. *Topoi*, **34**, 187–95.

Forbes, G. A. (2016). The growing block's past problems. *Philosophical Studies*, **173**, 699–709.

Forrest, P. (2004). The real but dead past: A reply to Braddon-Mitchell. *Analysis*, **64**, 358–62.

Frischhut, A. M. (2015). What experience cannot teach us about time. *Topoi*, **34**, 143–55.

Gale, R. M. (1968). *The Language of Time*. London: Routledge and Kegan Paul.

Gibson, I. & Pooley, O. (2008). Relativistic persistence. *Philosophical Perspectives (Metaphysics)*, **20**, 157–98.

Goldman, A. I. (2015). Naturalizing metaphysics with the help of cognitive science. In K. Bennett & D. W. Zimmerman, eds., *Oxford Studies in Metaphysics,* vol. 9. Oxford: Oxford University Press, pp. 171–213.

Goodman, N. (1951). *The Structure of Appearance*. Cambridge, MA: Harvard University Press.

Hawley, K. (2001). *How Things Persist*. Oxford: Oxford University Press.

Heil, J. (2005). *From an Ontological Point of View*. Oxford: Oxford University Press.

Heller, M. (1992). Things change. *Philosophy and Phenomenological Research*, **52**(3), 695–704.

Hestevold, H. S. (1990). Passage and the presence of experience. *Philosophy and Phenomenological Research*, **50**, 537–52.

Hinchliff, M. (1996). The puzzle of change. In J. E. Tomberlin ed., *Philosophical Perspectives 10, Metaphysics*. Oxford: Blackwell Publishers, pp. 119–36.

Hinchliff, M. (2000). A defense of presentism in a relativistic setting. *Philosophy of Science*, **67**, S575–86.

Hoerl, C. (2014). Do we (seem to) perceive passage?. *Philosophical Explorations*, **17**(2), 188–202.

Hoerl, C. & McCormack, T. (2019). Thinking in and about time: A dual systems perspective on temporal cognition. *Behavioral and Brain Sciences*, **42**, 1–69.

Ingthorsson, R. D. (2016). *McTaggart's Paradox*. New York: Routledge.

Ismael, J. (2011). Temporal experience. In C. Callender, ed., *The Oxford Handbook of Philosophy of Time*. Oxford: Oxford University Press, pp. 460–82.

Jackson, F. (1998). *From Metaphysics to Ethics: A Defence of Conceptual Analysis*. Oxford: Oxford University Press.

Kaplan, D. (1989). Demonstratives. In J. Almog, J. Perry & H. Wettstein, *Themes from Kaplan*. New York: Oxford University Press, pp. 481–563.

Kriegel, U. (2015). Experiencing the present. *Analysis*, **75**(3), 407–13.

Kripke, S. (1980). *Naming and Necessity*. Cambridge, MA: Harvard University Press.

Laplane, L., Mantovani, P., Adolphs, R., et al. (2019). Why science needs philosophy. *Proceedings of the National Academy of Sciences of the United States of America*, **116**, 3948–52.

Latham, A. J., Miller, K. & Norton, J. (2020a). Do the folk represent time as essentially dynamical?. *Inquiry*, https://doi.org/10.1080/0020174X.2020.1827027

Latham, A. J., Miller, K. & Norton, J. (2020b). An empirical investigation of purported passage phenomenology. *The Journal of Philosophy*, **117**, 353–86.

Latham, A. J., Miller, K. & Norton, J. (2021). Is our naïve theory of time dynamical?. *Synthese*, **198**, 4251–71

Leininger, L. (2014). On Mellor and the future direction of time. *Analysis*, **74** (1), 1–9.

Leininger, L. (2021). Temporal B-coming: Passage without presentness. *Australasian Journal of Philosophy*, **99**, 130–47 https://doi.org/10.1080/00048402.2020.1744673

Le Poidevin, R. D. (1991). *Change, Cause and Contradiction: A Defence of the Tenseless Theory of Time*. London: Palgrave Macmillan.

Le Poidevin, R. D. (2007). *The Images of Time*. Oxford: Oxford University Press.

Leslie, S.-J. (2013). Essence and natural kinds. In T. Gendler & J. Hawthorne, eds., *Oxford Studies in Epistemology*, vol. 4. Oxford: Oxford University Press, pp. 108–66.

Lipman, M. (2015). On Fine's fragmentalism. *Philosophical Studies*, **172**, 3119–33. https://doi.org/10.1007/s11098-015-0460-y

Lombard, L. (1999). On the alleged incompatibility of presentism and temporal parts. *Philosophia*, **27**, 253–60.

Lucas, J. R. (1973). *A Treatise on Time and Space*. London: Methuen.

Ludlow, P. (1999). *Semantics, Tense, and Time: An Essay in the Metaphysics of Natural Language*. Cambridge, MA: MIT Press.

MacBeath, M. (1986). Clipping time's wings, *Mind*, **95**, 233–37.

Maclaurin, J. & Dyke, H. (2002). 'Thank goodness that's over': The evolutionary story. *Ratio*, **15**, 276–92.

Markosian, N. (2004). A defense of presentism. In D. W. Zimmerman, ed., *Oxford Studies in Metaphysics*, vol. 1. Oxford: Oxford University Press, pp. 47–82.

McTaggart, J. M. E. (1908). The Unreality of Time, *Mind*, **17**, 457–73.

McTaggart, J. M. E. (1927). *The Nature of Existence*, vol. 2. Cambridge: Cambridge University Press.

Mellor, D. H. (1981). *Real Time*. Cambridge: Cambridge University Press.

Mellor, D. H. (1998). *Real Time II*. London: Routledge.

Mellor, D. H. (2013). *Mind, Meaning, and Reality: Essays in Philosophy*. Oxford: Oxford University Press.

Meyer, U. (2005). The presentist's dilemma. *Philosophical Studies*, **122**(3), 213–25.

Miller, K. (2013). Presentism, eternalism, and the growing block. In H. Dyke & A. Bardon, eds., *A Companion to the Philosophy of Time*. Malden, MA: Wiley-Blackwell, pp. 345–64.

Miller, K. & Norton, J. (2021). If time can pass, time can pass at different rates. *Analytic Philosophy*, **62**(1), 21–32.

Monton, B. (2010). McTaggart and modern physics. *Philosophia*, **38**, 257–64.

Mozersky, M. J. (2013). The B-theory in the twentieth century. In H. Dyke and A. Bardon, eds., *A Companion to the Philosophy of Time*. Malden, MA: Wiley-Blackwell, pp. 167–82.

Mozersky, M. J. (2015). *Time, Language and Ontology: The World from the B-theoretic Perspective*. Oxford: Oxford University Press.

Nagel, T. (1989). *The View from Nowhere*. Oxford: Oxford University Press.

Norton, J. D. (2010). Time really passes. *Humana. Mente Journal of Philosophical Studies*, **4**(13), 23–34.

Oaklander, L. N. (1984). *Temporal Relations and Temporal Becoming: A Defense of a Russellian Theory of Time*. Lanham, MD: University Press of America.

Oaklander, L. N. (2004). *The Ontology of Time*. New York: Prometheus.

Oaklander, L. N. (2010). McTaggart's paradox and Crisp's presentism. *Philosophia*, **38**, 229–41.

Oaklander, L. N. (2012). A-, B-, and R-theories of time: A debate. In A. Bardon, ed. *The Future of the Philosophy of Time*. London: Routledge, pp. 1–24.

Olson, E. T. (2009). The rate of time's passage. *Analysis*, **69**(1), 3–8.

Paul, L. A. (2010). Temporal experience. *The Journal of Philosophy*, **107**(7), 333–59.

Penrose, R. (1989). *The Emperor's New Mind: Concerning Computers, Minds, and the Laws of Physics*. Oxford: Oxford University Press.

Perry, J. (1979). The problem of the essential indexical. *Noûs*, **13**, 3–21.

Phillips, I. (2009). Rate abuse: A reply to Olson. *Analysis*, **69**(3), 503–05.

Pooley, O. (2013). Relativity, the open future, and the passage of time. *Proceedings of the Aristotelian Society*, **113**(3), 321–63.

Power, S. E. (2018). *Philosophy of Time and Perceptual Experience*. New York: Routledge.

Price, H. (1996). *Time's Arrow and Archimedes' Point: New Directions for the Physics of Time*. Oxford: Oxford University Press.

Price, H. (2011). The flow of time. In C. Callender, ed., *The Oxford Handbook of Philosophy of Time*. Oxford: Oxford University Press, pp. 276–311.

Prior, A. N. (1959). Thank goodness that's over. *Philosophy*, **34**(128), 12–17.

Prior, A. N. (1967). *Past, Present and Future*. Oxford: Oxford University Press.

Prior, A. N. (1968). Changes in events and changes in things. In A. N. Prior, ed., *Papers on Time and Tense*. Oxford: Oxford University Press, pp. 1–14.

Prior, A. N. (1970). The notion of the present. *Studium Generale*, **23**, 245–48.

Prosser, S. (2007). Could we experience the passage of time? *Ratio*, **20**, 75–90.

Prosser, S. (2013). Passage and perception. *Noûs*, **47**(1), 69–84

Prosser, S. (2016). *Experiencing Time*. Oxford: Oxford University Press.

Putnam, H. (1967). Time and physical geometry. *The Journal of Philosophy*, **64**(8), 240–47.

Putnam, H. (1975). The meaning of meaning. In H. Putnam, ed., *Mind, Language and Reality*. Cambridge: Cambridge University Press, pp. 215–71.

Quine, W. V. O. (1960). *Word and Object*. Cambridge, MA: MIT Press.

Rea, M. C. (2003). Four-dimensionalism. In M. J. Loux & D. W. Zimmerman, eds., *The Oxford Handbook of Metaphysics*. Oxford: Oxford University Press, pp. 246–80.

Raven, M. (2011). Can time pass at the rate of 1 second per second? *Australasian Journal of Philosophy*, **89**(3), 459–65.

Rietdijk, C. W. (1966). A rigorous proof of determinism derived from the special theory of relativity. *Philosophy of Science*, **33**(4), 341–44.

Riggs, P. J. (2017). The perceptions and experience of the 'passage' of time. *The Philosophical Forum*, **48**(1), 3–30.

Rovelli, C. (2018). Physics needs philosophy. Philosophy needs physics. *Foundations of Physics*, **48**, 481–91.

Russell, B. (1915). On the experience of time. *The Monist*, **25**(2), 212–33.

Russell, B. (1938). *Principles of Mathematics*. New York: W. W. Norton.

Ryle, G. (1954). It was to be. In G. Ryle, ed., *Dilemmas: The Tanner Lectures*. Cambridge: Cambridge University Press, pp. 15–35.

Saunders, S. (2002). How relativity contradicts presentism. In C. Callender, ed., *Time, Reality and Experience*. Royal Institute of Philosophy Supplement, **50**. Cambridge: Cambridge University Press, pp. 277–92.

Savitt, S. (2002). On absolute becoming and the myth of passage. *Royal Institute of Philosophy Supplement*, **50**, 153–67.

Savitt, S. (2006). Presentism and eternalism in perspective. In D. Dieks, ed., *The Ontology of Spacetime*. Oxford: Elsevier, pp. 111–27.

Schlesinger, G. N. (1982). How time flies. *Mind*, **91**, 501–23.

Schlesinger, G. N. (1991). E pur si muove. *The Philosophical Quarterly*, **41**(165), 427–41.

Schlesinger, G. N. (1994). *Timely Topics*. Basingstoke: Macmillan Press.

Schuster, M. M. (1986). Is the flow of time subjective? *The Review of Metaphysics*, **39**(4), 695–714.

Shardlow, J., Lee, R., Hoerl, C. et al., (2021). Exploring people's beliefs about the experience of time. *Synthese*, **198**, 10709–31 https://doi.org/10.1007/s11229-020-02749-2

Sider, T. (1999). Presentism and ontological commitment. *The Journal of Philosophy*, **96**(7), 325–47.

Sider, T. (2001). *Four-dimensionalism*. Oxford: Oxford University Press.

Sider, T. (2006). Quantifiers and temporal ontology. *Mind*, **115**(457), 75–97.

Sinha, C. & Gärdenfors, P. (2014). Time, space, and events in language and cognition: a comparative view. *Annals of the New York Academy of Sciences, Issue: Flow of Time*, **40**, 1–10.

Skow, B. (2011a). On the meaning of the question 'how fast does time pass? *Philosophical Studies*, **155**, 325–44.

Skow, B. (2011b). Experience and the passage of time. *Philosophical Perspectives*, **25**(1), 359–87.

Skow, B. (2015). *Objective Becoming*. Oxford: Oxford University Press.

Smart, J. J. C. (1949). The river of time. *Mind*, **58**(232), 483–94.

Smart, J. J. C. (1963). *Philosophy and Scientific Realism*. London: Routledge and Kegan Paul.

Smart, J. J. C. (1980). Time and becoming. In P. van Inwagen, ed., *Time and Cause*. Dordrecht: D. Reidel, pp. 3–15.

Smith, N. J. J. (2011). Inconsistency in the A-theory. *Philosophical Studies*, **156**, 231–47.

Smith, Q. (1993). *Language and Time*. Oxford: Oxford University Press.

Smith, Q. (1994). The phenomenology of A-time. In L. N. Oaklander & Q. Smith, eds., *The New Theory of Time*. New Haven: Yale University Press, pp. 351–59.

Sprigge, T. L. S. (1992). The unreality of time. *Proceedings of the Aristotelian Society*, **92**, 1–19.

Suhler, C. & Callender, C. (2012). Thank goodness that argument is over: Explaining the temporal value asymmetry. *Philosopher's Imprint*, **12**(15), 1–16.

Tallant, J. (2010a). Time for presence? *Philosophia*, **38**, 271–80.

Tallant, J. (2010b). Sketch of a presentist theory of passage, *Erkenntnis*, **73**, 133–40.

Tallant, J. (2016). Temporal passage and the 'no alternate possibilities' argument, *Manuscrito*, **39**(4), 35–47.

Taylor, K. (2019). *Meaning Diminished: Toward Metaphysically Modest Semantics*. Oxford: Oxford University Press.

Tooley, M. (1997). *Time, Tense and Causation*. Oxford: Oxford University Press.

Torre, S. (2010). Tense, timely action and self-ascription. *Philosophy and Phenomenological Research*, **80**(1), 112–32.

Torrengo, G. (2017). Feeling the passing of time. *The Journal of Philosophy*, **114**(4), 165–88.

Torrengo, G. (2018). Perspectival tenses and dynamic tenses. *Erkenntnis*, **83**, 1045–61.

Williams, B. (1978). *Descartes*. Harmondsworth: Penguin.

Williams, D. C. (1951). The myth of passage. *The Journal of Philosophy*, **48**, 457–72.

Zimmerman, D. W. (2005). The A-theory of time, the B-theory of time and 'taking tense seriously'. *Dialectica*, **59**, 401–57.

Zimmerman, D. W. (2008). The privileged present: Defending an 'A-theory' of time. In T. Sider, J. Hawthorne & D. Zimmerman, eds., *Contemporary Debates in Metaphysics*. Oxford: Blackwell, pp. 211–25.

Acknowledgements

I am deeply grateful to two anonymous referees for Cambridge University Press, to Adrian Bardon, Craig Callender, Robin Le Poidevin, Kristie Miller and Josh Mozersky, and to audiences at departmental seminars at the Universities of Waikato and Otago, and at the Australasian Association of Philosophy online Conference 2021, who all gave me constructive and insightful comments on the first draft of this Element. I also want to thank Tuomas Tahko, the Metaphysics series editor, for having the confidence in me to invite me to write it. Heartfelt thanks also to my family, Ian, Ruby and Damian, for giving me the time and space to write, and for ensuring that time not spent writing is always filled with happiness and laughter. At the start of the project, I ran the proposal past my dear friend and 'grand-supervisor' Hugh Mellor. I'm happy to say he liked it, but so very sad that he didn't live to read the published version. I dedicate it to him.

Cambridge Elements ☰

Metaphysics

Tuomas E. Tahko

University of Bristol

Tuomas E. Tahko is Professor of Metaphysics of Science at the University of Bristol, UK. Tahko specialises in contemporary analytic metaphysics, with an emphasis on methodological and epistemic issues: 'meta-metaphysics'. He also works at the interface of metaphysics and philosophy of science: 'metaphysics of science'. Tahko is the author of *Unity of Science* (CUP, 2021, *Elements in Philosophy of Science*), *An Introduction to Metametaphysics* (CUP, 2015) and editor of *Contemporary Aristotelian Metaphysics* (CUP, 2012).

About the Series

This highly accessible series of Elements provides brief but comprehensive introductions to the most central topics in metaphysics. Many of the Elements also go into considerable depth, so the series will appeal to both students and academics. Some Elements bridge the gaps between metaphysics, philosophy of science and epistemology.

Cambridge Elements$^{\equiv}$

Metaphysics

Elements in the Series

Relations
John Heil

Material Objects
Thomas Sattig

Time
Heather Dyke

A full series listing is available at: www.cambridge.org/EMPH

CPSIA information can be obtained
at www.ICGtesting.com
Printed in the USA
BVHW042004151221
624126BV00012B/277